## Are you...

- Preparing for a leadership position and craving a roadmap so you can start out strong?

- Confronting the joys and difficulties in your first years of leadership?

- Looking for ideas to expand your skills and revitalize your passion for the work?

- Wishing you understood what your colleagues think and why they do what they do?

- Studying business, longing for a primer that offers practical help?

- Searching for group leadership materials to train, motivate, and inspire?

- Committed to supporting leaders you know in their worthy endeavors?

*Be a Great Leader by Friday* is exactly what you're looking for. Whether you are pursuing business, community, family, or any other arena, this book is filled with practical wisdom, time-tested principles, and inspiration for aspiring and already-in-the-trenches leaders to be and do their personal best.

In just five days you'll master leadership basics, identify your strengths and weaknesses, and discover how to take the best advantage of both. You'll learn how to maximize relationships with those you serve and who serve with you and craft your unique culture that will motivate your colleagues, assist with problem-solving, and provide a win-win community for all. You'll grow and refine leadership traits and strategies, while feeling a sense of fulfillment and accomplishing a work-home balance.

The winning plays in this book will prepare and energize you to positively impact your colleagues and clients. But that's not all. Your newfound knowledge, skills, and confidence will benefit you anywhere you roam. What's not to like about that bang for your buck?

Simply turn the page to spark your world-changing potential.

You'll be glad you did.

# Be a
# Great
# Leader
## by Friday

## 5 Winning Plays
## to Spark Your
## World-Changing Potential

# Dr. Kevin Leman

**BroadStreet**
PUBLISHING

BroadStreet Publishing ® Group, LLC
Savage, Minnesota, USA
BroadStreetPublishing.com

*Be a Great Leader by Friday: 5 Winning Plays to Spark Your World-Changing Potential*

9781424568321 (hardcover)
9781424568338 (ebook)

Editors: Ramona Cramer Tucker, Michelle Winger

To protect the privacy of those who have shared their stories with the authors, details and names have been changed.

Stock or custom editions of BroadStreet Publishing titles may be purchased in bulk for educational, business, ministry, fundraising, or sales promotional use. For information, please email orders@ broadstreetpublishing.com.

Cover and interior by Garborg Design Works| garborgdesign.com

Printed in China
24 25 26 27 28 5 4 3 2 1

*This book is affectionately dedicated to
Dennis Michael O'Reilly,
the epitome of a great leader.*

*He listens well, expects the best and gets the best,
defers credit to others, gives them a second chance,
and holds them to the highest standards.*

*His dedication to his craft
and to relationships with teachers,
parents, and scholars is unparalleled,
garnering their deep respect.*

*Dennis wrote the original charter for
The Leman Academy of Excellence
with his wife, Krissy.
He served as the first principal
at the original Marana campus,
and was the stellar Head of Schools
who led the Academy to its award-winning status.*

*It has been my privilege to watch his leadership
and all those who have prospered as a result.*

*Dennis, I hope you take personal pride
in your accomplishments
and the continuing legacy of a job well done.*

# Contents

## It's All About the Three Rs

*Your opportunity to positively impact
your spheres of influence starts right now.*

Want to impact the world for good? You can! And as a leader, you have the unparalleled opportunity to do that every single day.

Whether you are neck-deep in being a new leader, a veteran with lots of stories to tell, taking classes in business, or considering pursuing a leadership position, there is something you need to know. Leadership isn't just a job. Neither is it only a position or title. If that's all it is to you, you won't stay a leader for long. Leadership is a lot of hard work. Sitting on the sidelines and letting others take the lead is far easier.

Instead, leadership is *personal*. It's a mindset that highlights relationships, welcomes expanding skills, and grasps the unparalleled opportunity to be a change-maker. No matter the arena of leadership you pursue, this book will provide you with the practical information and inspirational motivation you need to become a successful leader.

If I asked you to summarize your goal(s) as a leader in one sentence, what would you say? For many, that would be a tough exercise because likely many goals fight for attention in your head. But if you and I talked for even 10 minutes, I have no doubt we'd zero in on your most important goal. A goal, in fact, that every single leader on the planet shares.

> Leadership is *personal.* It's a mindset that highlights relationships, welcomes expanding skills, and grasps the unparalleled opportunity to be a change-maker.

Talk to leaders anywhere, and you'll find they're all looking to do the same thing: *motivate their people to do the best job possible.* Along the way, if they are in business, leaders also want to expand their contacts and make some money. If they are community leaders, they want to start and finish projects well and stretch their circle of influence. If they are leaders in their homes, they want to do the right thing for all family members and forge beneficial relationships that will stand the test of time and weather.

How exactly do you motivate those you serve and who serve with you to do the best job possible? It's all about the 3 Rs: **R**elationships, **R**elationships, **R**elationships.

Yes, you read that right.

Relationships are so important to leaders that I've repeated the word three times. Beneficial, productive relationships with colleagues, customers, and anyone else you come in contact with at work, home, and in your community are critical to your success as a leader. Therefore, you'll find the important thread of relationships running throughout this book.

Why are the 3 Rs so important? It's simple. If you don't understand people, you won't get anywhere close to accomplishing your goals. That's why I believe every leader needs to be a psychologist of sorts. The more you understand about how humans "work" and why they do what they do, the more equipped you'll be as a leader in *any* sphere of influence. Your unparalleled opportunity to make a positive impact starts with understanding and relating to people.

## What I Learned Peddling Magazines

The idea that knowing basic psychology is valuable to business and leadership dawned on me when I was…*not* in college.

It was spring, and I'd arrived in Tucson, Arizona, after doing not so well at a small college in the Midwest. By not so well, I mean I somehow managed to pull off a C average during my freshman year by making use of the fear factor, *aka,* fear of having to go to work. However, even that motivation tanked sophomore year, and I started flunking courses.

> Talk to leaders anywhere, and you'll find they're all looking to do the same thing: *motivate their people to do the best job possible.*

My college career ended swiftly when my jokester side took control too strongly, and I pulled the ultimate no-no prank. I stole the "Conscience Fund" from my dorm for a laugh. The college dean wasn't amused. We had a short-but-not-too-sweet exchange. I left that office with a very firm invitation to leave school permanently.

What would I do next? I had no idea. My parents had recently moved to Tucson to escape the bitter winters of Buffalo, New York, so I hightailed it in that direction. I figured at least then I'd have somewhere to sleep and Mom's cooking while I figured things out.

The only work I could find in Tucson was a janitorial job at a medical center, working full-time at such a low wage that it barely covered my gas and other minimal expenses. It didn't take me long to reason, *This isn't what I want to do with my life. Maybe I'd better give college another shot.* This time I decided on the University of Arizona. But how would I get the money?

I landed a job selling magazines door-to-door. My intensive training lasted all of one afternoon. Here's the strategy I learned. You walked up to the front door, smiled, and gave a basic pitch. "Hi! You're probably very busy, but could I take a minute of your time? We're conducting research for a nationally known firm, and we're in your neighborhood today. We'd like you to tell us which four magazines on this list you'd like to have absolutely free."

If the person took that card listing dozens of magazines and started looking at it, you knew you had a chance. And if that customer actually picked four magazines she wanted "absolutely free," you knew you almost had a sale. But there was a catch. You had to get the front money—the down payment on three more magazine subscriptions that the customer had to buy in order to get the other four free.

The training taught you to say, "That's right. It's only $7 down and $2.95 a month." This was 1962, so the prices were a little different. What we were told *not* to mention was that the customer would pay $2.95 a month for 26 months. Do some simple math, and you'll realize that's an additional $76.70 to that $7. That meant the customer was really paying $83.70 for the seven magazine subscriptions—the three she was buying and the four "free" ones.

> I landed a job selling magazines door-to-door. My intensive training lasted all of one afternoon.

There's nothing new about that kind of approach. It's called getting suckers to buy on impulse. You aren't exactly lying, but you aren't giving them all the information either. And they still are getting a good deal: seven magazines for about 12 dollars a year per magazine.

Keep in mind that $83.70 wasn't exactly cheap in 1962, so peddling magazines like that was often a tough sell. It was even more so when a customer had enough sense to ask, "$2.95

a month for *how many* months?" But I needed a job, even with the odds against me of finding customers who could be fooled by the "get four free and buy three more" sales technique.

The next morning I reported back to the company for my first day at work. I was driven out to a middle-class neighborhood, dumped on a corner, and told to be back there for pickup by 1:00 p.m. I knocked on doors and followed the script as I'd been told. The morning flew by as I collected orders.

Back at the office, I handed the sheaf of papers to my supervisor. I felt like I'd done well, but I was anxious about what she would say. She took one look and asked, "What are *these*?"

"They're my orders," I said nervously, wondering if I'd failed the test.

"You mean you got *all* these orders this morning?" she asked incredulously.

I smiled sheepishly. "Yep."

"Come with me," she said. We walked back to the manager's office. "Look!" she called to the manager, "Look at what Calvin did!"

My 27 orders for magazines, I found out, was not only a one-morning record for that office but for the entire company nationwide. I was feeling so good that I didn't even bother to correct that supervisor on my name.

What was the secret to my success in peddling magazines? Looking back, I believe four things were in my favor.

First, a lot of my customers were stay-at-home wives and moms. Likely they felt sorry for the nice youngster in the U. of A. T-shirt sweating on their doorstep and trying to explain about the really wonderful opportunity.

Second, I had a knack for spotting approachable individuals. Since crime then wasn't like it is today, I'd get them to invite me in. Soon I'd wind up in the living room with the lady of the house apologizing for the mess. After assuring her the house looked lovely and I was happy to be there, I was usually offered lemonade or coffee.

Third, I was very service oriented, even before I realized what that concept meant. I'd always ask if I could help with anything while I was there. My mother and sister, Sally, eight years my senior, had trained me well to be helpful.

Fourth, I was positive and relational. I wasn't the threatening, huff-and-puff, blow-them-down sales type. I'd push for a decision, but I was never pushy. I'd go for a soft sell. And I put on my dancin' shoes. All my life I'd made friends easily. I could make people laugh when there didn't seem to be anything to laugh about.

---

**LEMANISM #1**

Be positive, relational,
and service oriented.

---

Little did I know then that my lastborn personality—something you'll learn about in this book—gave me an edge for sales. As the last child born in my family, I knew I could never compete with my straight-A big sister or stellar-in-athletics big brother. So I did something I *could* excel at. Nicknamed "Cub" by my parents when I was only 11 days old, I fulfilled that role. I became the family mascot, clown, and comedian.

Making friends easily and making people laugh was helpful in business too, I discovered. While selling magazines, I once approached a door with a sign: UNLESS YOU'RE A FRIEND, DON'T KNOCK ON THIS DOOR. Naturally, because I'm me, I went ahead and knocked on the door.

A sleepy looking man answered. He looked as if I'd launched him off his couch. He tossed a sour look and a "Yeah?" question my way.

*This doesn't seem to be a good sales situation,* I told myself. So, swallowing hard, I talked fast: "Oh, hi, sir. I just read your sign. I had no way of knowing if you were a friend until I took a look at you."

For several long seconds, the man stared at me. Then he sighed. We had a brief exchange. He didn't buy any magazines. But when he shut the door, he was chuckling. I considered that a personal win, even if it wasn't a financial one.

## A Conscience Kicks in for the Kid Who Stole the "Conscience Fund"

After my record first day, I sold subscriptions for several more weeks, continuing to do well. Then something started to bother me. Yes, I was a success. I was bringing in a lot of orders and making some decent money for a college kid.

But within two months, I knew I had made a mistake. My gut told me this deal was too slick. I was using my natural abilities to take advantage of people. That's when I realized I had a conscience because it was stabbing me relentlessly.

The next day I walked into the dreary apartment that served as the magazine sales office and told my supervisor I was quitting. "But why?" she asked. "You're the best salesperson we've got. You're doing great, and you're only a kid."

When I told her why, she cocked her head, looked at me for a minute, and then shrugged. "Sorry to lose you, Kevin. You're really good. A natural-born salesperson."

I walked out that door with mixed emotions. Happy that she'd finally remembered my name correctly. Worried about finding another job that would pay as well as that tough gig. Glad I'd found something that I was good at—sales. Deep down, I knew I was making the right decision even though I had no idea what the future held.

It is what you learn
after you know it all that counts.

JOHN WOODEN, AMERICAN BASKETBALL COACH

## What I Learned about What Matters Most

I will forever be grateful for peddling magazines at such a formative time. Through that experience I learned the basics of five valuable leadership principles.

First, I discovered that I was a natural-born salesperson and very good at it. The only person (other than my mother, God bless her) who had told me that I had skills I could use for good was a high school teacher, Ms. Eleanor Wilson. That was after my antics had exasperated nearly every other teacher and staff member in the entire school. While peddling magazines, I realized my birth order figured greatly into those innate skills. I was groomed for sales and being in the limelight from babyhood onward.

Second, I uncovered the type of person I *didn't* want to be. That was someone who took advantage of others. I knew I needed to walk away from a venture that pricked my conscience. From that day onward, I would never use my natural sales talent to slicker people. Instead I'd ensure that whatever I did would provide a *service,* something of real *value* to others, and that I would always offer it with the right motive. Sure, I would have to figure out a way to make a living, but I'd never again try to slip a deal past my customers to make a buck.

### LEMANISM #2

There has to be more to making money
than making money.

Third, I realized that getting to know my customers as individuals, rather than simply viewing them as potential sales, was important. I had to know who I was selling to, who I was working with, and who was working for me. I had to view the world from behind their eyes, see with their perspective. I had to win their cooperation—not coerce or fool them to get on board.

Fourth, I needed a clear-cut purpose and refined strategies. I needed to be intentional about setting goals and relaying the mission to every colleague I worked with and every customer I interacted with. I needed to create the kind of environment I'd want to work in myself. It had to be the kind of respectful, safe, and energetic workplace that would grow my colleagues' skills along with their hearts.

Fifth, I could not sell a vision without living it out myself in every arena of life. I had to follow my own moral compass. I had to set priorities that would balance home and work and never waver from them, despite potential financial or career loss. I had to remember to take breaks to refuel when I needed them. I had to live out the concept that failure is a natural part of life, but it can become the ladder to success with a winning attitude.

### *Thoughts of a Successful Leader*

Our greatest weakness lies in giving up.
The most certain way to succeed
is always to try just one more time.

THOMAS EDISON, AMERICAN INVENTOR

Each of these five basic principles took on more depth as I proceeded to fine-tune my leadership opportunities, skills, traits, and strategies. I now had a purpose: to serve and empower people to be the best version of themselves. My life had meaning and value because that is what I was determined to give others.

Now it was time to fulfill my goals. My motivation kicked in, and I got serious about my studies. I went on to get my bachelor's, master's, and doctorate degrees, all from the University of Arizona. While studying psychology, I learned how a human's personality is formed, the powerful influences that play an important role, and how those factors impact how a person thinks and acts.

By the end of those studies, I became even more convinced that when you understand others' needs, desires, and what matters most to them, and you assist them in fulfilling those, there isn't anything you can't accomplish together. That's true of you too.

## It's Your Time

Want to be a great leader by Friday? You can, and this book will help you get there. *Be a Great Leader by Friday* combines real-life psychology with time-tested principles for success. It provides a win-win approach to manage and work with others in ways that will accomplish your mission, fuel your passion and purpose, and grow your arena of influence. It will help you motivate and empower your colleagues to do their personal bests.

I've shared the concepts in this book for decades with CEOs and other business leaders across the globe as well as organizational, faith-based, and family leaders. Now I'm sharing it with you. I can't wait to see what you do with it or the places you'll go.

So let's make a deal, shall we? No matter the arena of your leadership, just give me five days. In those few days you will:

- Discover your strengths and how to take best advantage of any weaknesses.

- Refine your leadership traits and increase your management skills.

- Explore why people do what they do and how to uniquely motivate them.

- Get comfortable with win-win relational principles to help you start and finish strong with *anyone* in *any* sphere of influence.

- Learn strategies that will put you in the driver's seat and ensure that the people you serve and who serve with you are on the right seat of your bus.

- Intentionally craft a unique culture that matches your goals, assists with problem-solving, and provides a beneficial work community that's both safe and energizing.

- Uncover the secrets to managing that often-elusive work-home balance like a pro. Do so, and you'll be able to stand strong in any wind that might blow your way, personal or professional.

Along the way, we'll pack in some bonus materials, including "Thoughts of a Successful Leader" from those who have been through the trials of leadership, "Lemanisms," nugget-sized memorable truths to tuck in your back pocket for when you need them most, and "Work It Out" to help you view situations, people, and problems through a new lens.

The "Top 15 Countdown for Leaders" on page 171 provides an easy wrap-up of key concepts you'll learn in this book. You might even want to post a copy where you can see them every day.

All those perks are only for starters. There's so much more.

Are you ready to zero in on your purpose, boost your passion, and reveal your world-changing potential?

Let's do it together.

### Thoughts of a Successful Leader

Always remember, you have within you
the strength, the patience, and the passion
to reach for the stars to change the world.

HARRIET TUBMAN, AMERICAN ABOLITIONIST
AND SOCIAL ACTIVIST

## Winning Play #1
## Know Yourself, Maximize Your Strengths

*Heighten your leadership potential*
*by understanding why you do what you do*

I was in the green room of a TV talk show, waiting to go on the air, when a billionaire business leader swept into the room with his entourage. He was scheduled to appear for the six minutes right before me talking about, of all things, the principles of leadership success. I was holding a copy of my *Birth Order Book,* the subject I'd been asked to talk about.

"What's birth order?" the billionaire wanted to know.

I smiled. I knew from experience that the best way to introduce anyone to birth order was to guess their birth order from what I observed about them in only a few minutes. So I said, "Well, you're probably an only child, aren't you?"

He looked at me rather strangely. "Why, yes…but how did you know?"

That was the beginning of our energetic discussion. The billionaire was extremely detailed and clearly a high achiever. His mind was a proverbial steel trap. He was organized, time-conscious, and targeted in his interactions. His facial expressions, body language, and the intentionality I'd observed in his actions were typical of an only child.

But that day he did something atypical. After his spot on the air, instead of hustling with his entourage into the limo to head for the airport, he announced to them, "Everybody sit down. Dr. Leman is on next, and we're going to learn something about birth order."

They were still there when I finished with my segment. I'll never forget what that business leader told me. "You know, that makes sense. Big business and industry would be smart to pay attention to everyone's birth order, especially when assigning certain jobs within the organization." Within a few minutes, that only child had not only grasped the concept of birth order but had synthesized what he'd learned into his business model.

Understanding birth order and applying it to yourself and others is critical to being a great leader by Friday. It will help you win people over and make them *allies* instead of simply people who work with you because you hired them, or they were assigned to work under you. It will encourage and motivate your customers to keep coming back for more because they feel that you actually care about them, not merely the sale.

The number-one topic that Fortune 500 companies, work groups like Million Dollar Round Table, the Top of the Table, the Young Presidents' Organization, and other professional organizations ask me to talk about is birth order. Why? Because once you understand birth order, your success track record will be high. When colleagues begin to see how it works and what they can gain from knowing about it, even those short on sleep or motivation suddenly pay attention.

Why do they care? Because such information is not only intriguing, it's personal and relational. It also has everything to do with professional growth. What you learn will make the difference between success and failure in leadership.

When you understand birth order, you'll be better equipped to discern others' strengths and weaknesses, so you can transition them to roles they're best suited for. You'll be able to uniquely motivate them by knowing how to forge the best path for a beneficial connection. Doing so will create a positive work environment that's a winning community for all. Without those people solidly in your court, any success you might attain will be temporary.

> Once you understand birth order, your success track record will be high.

Imagine an environment where colleagues fight to join your team because it's not only known for tackling big projects with excellence, but each team member feels included and appreciated. They have a leader who actually thanks them for their work and has their back. Who wouldn't be attracted to that team like a fly to honey? Your retention rate will go through the roof. You'll be the company every other company wants to emulate.

Yes, that can be you after this five-day journey we'll take together.

But first things first. When you're a leader, the first person you need to understand completely is *you*. How do you operate the best? How will you use your strengths and shore up your weaknesses? If you don't know and understand *you,* you won't be able to lead others effectively because you won't be able to understand *them.*

That's why, in this book, we start with getting to know yourself even better than you already do. You must know not only *what* you are doing but *why* you are doing it. By the time you finish this chapter, you'll have a good understanding of what makes you and others tick. That understanding will pay big dividends in every arena of influence.

**LEMANISM #3**
Know yourself first,
before you stick your nose in others' business.

## What Is Birth Order?

What exactly is "birth order," and why is it important? Stated simply, birth order is the science of understanding your particular limb on the family tree. The order in which a child is born or adopted into a family has a significant impact on his or her thoughts, actions, and worldview.

It was Alfred Adler, the founder of Individual Psychology, who first talked decades ago about each person's place in what he called the "Family Constellation." His theory was that "different positions in a family birth order may be correlated to positive and negative life outcomes."[1] Much has happened since the early days of Adler's work. I'm convinced he got some specifics right and others quite wrong.

For example, Adler was a middle child—not born first, and not born last—so he considered that position optimal.[2] I've talked to a lot of middleborns who wouldn't share that perspective. They've felt like the frosting in a cookie sandwich all their lives, squished on both sides. Yet look at what middleborns such as Bill Gates, Mark Zuckerberg, Jennifer Lopez, Michael Jordan, Katy Perry, Chris Hemsworth, and Anne Hathaway have accomplished.

Adler considered firstborns "neurotic" due to their perceived roles, responsibilities, and excessive seeking of adult approval, especially when "dethroned once a sibling comes along."[3] He theorized only children are deficient, useless, and can't be independent due to a lack of peer socialization and rivals for their parents' affection, which leads to pampering and spoiling.[4] But think for a minute. Is this true of all firstborns and onlies? No. In fact, where would we be without these people?

Today a lot of accountants, scientists, astronauts, doctors, and dentists are firstborns and onlies. Would you want an accountant who says, "I think you owe a couple thousand to the IRS, give or take a thousand?" No, you need an exact number, down to the cents, to bequeath to the government. Would you want a dentist who admits, "Oops, I pulled the wrong incisor"? I'm cowardly when it comes to anything medical. Before I even get in that dentist's chair, I ask, "You're a firstborn or only child, am I right?"

Firstborn leaders include U.S. Presidents Bill Clinton (42nd), George W. Bush (43rd), Barack Obama (44th), and Joseph R. Biden Jr. (46th), as well as Oprah Winfrey, Hillary Clinton, and J.K. Rowling. Famous only children include Adele, Leonardo DiCaprio, Justin Timberlake, Selena Gomez, Alicia Keys, Robert De Niro, Drew Barrymore, and Natalie Portman.

Adler also felt that lastborns tended to be grandiose, wanting to be "bigger than the others," with "huge plans that never work out," due to having too many mothers and fathers (*aka,* older siblings).[5] Famous lastborns such as Celine Dion, Cameron Diaz, Serena Williams, Mark Wahlberg, and Julia Roberts have certainly proven that prediction wrong.

Each birth order has special roles and ways to contribute. Each is needed to make the world go 'round.

## Looking Through the Eyes of the Birth Orders

Birth order isn't an exact science, and Adler's writings aren't easy reading. In fact, they're clear as mud in places and leave lots of room for interpretation. However, what's most important is his main idea: that birth order is vital to understanding how each person in a family interprets their environment. It explains why siblings can have vastly differing views of the same event.

> Birth order is the science of understanding your particular limb on the family tree.

Sarai grew up with hard-working parents who struggled to make ends meet. One year was especially tough in pinching pennies. Her "new" clothes were hand-me-downs from cousins or thrift-store finds. The family ate lots of homemade soup and stretch-the-meat casseroles. Family "outings" were going out to their postage-stamp-size backyard.

Over a recent holiday meal, she and her two siblings reminisced about that time. She couldn't believe how differently they interpreted the same facts.

Sarai said she felt tense and anxious. She wondered if their family was going to be okay. She wished she were older so she could work and make some money to help out.

To her brother, it was no different than other years, except he couldn't get ice cream at the corner store with friends on Fridays after school. At home, he only wanted everyone to be happy and get along. When things got stressful, he'd hide out in that backyard for a while.

Sarai's other sister fondly recalls that time as a highlight. They did so many activities as a family. She enthusiastically talks about the night they camped out under the stars in tents made with old blankets. They roasted marshmallows on sticks over a small pit built from rocks they all collected. She concocted a play and roped in the whole family to act it out. The siblings who typically didn't give her the time of day, except for an occasional eye roll at her antics, paid attention to her. Everyone was laughing, and she got to be the hub of the fun.

> Each birth order has special roles and ways to contribute.

Birth order explains those differing perspectives of the same event. You'll soon see how and why. Then you'll get your own chance to "Work It Out" by guessing the birth order of those siblings from what you've learned. Won't that be fun?

For now, let's look directly at you. Were you born first, second, third, or even farther down the line in your family? Are you an only child? Were you adopted into a family who already had other children? No matter your position as a limb on the family tree, your birth order has influenced your life in countless ways.

That's why, to truly know yourself and the potential you are capable of, you need to understand your own birth order and the inherent strengths and weaknesses that come with each birth order. As we take a quick trip through the birth orders, keep in mind that not every strength or weakness may apply to you. No individual has *all* of the typical characteristics attributed to his or her birth order.

> Birth order is vital to understanding how each person in a family interprets their environment.

Each of us is a unique blend of characteristics, personality traits, environmental factors, and other variables. These variables include the gender of children, the spacing between their entry into the family via birth or adoption, and the blending of families. Physical, emotional, or mental differences between children or the death of a child can also prompt a younger child to usurp an older child's position. All of these factors, along with your birth order, contribute to the full picture of who you are. For more intrigue on the subject, see my *Birth Order Book*.[6] For the purposes of this chapter, we'll focus on your interpretation of your position in the family and how that impacts your thoughts and actions.

Which of the following sounds most like you?

### The Firstborn

You were the rockstar, the oldest kid in your family. You talked first, walked first, and entered school first. Your parents were stricter with you than with your siblings. That's because you were the guinea pig in their parenting experiment. They used you to help set the high bar of example for any other children who might follow.

As the role model constantly in the limelight for your siblings, you didn't feel all that special. You lived constantly with pressure. Your parents pinned their eagle eyes on you. You had to do extra chores because they knew you'd get them done. You were always the responsible one called upon to organize your siblings, make their lunches when your parents were at work, and feed the family dog. On top of that, you had to keep up your grades and top-dog position at school so you wouldn't get eaten alive in the peer jungle.

When you got home, you didn't have a minute's peace. Those pesky siblings were always in your face and space, ruining your treasured possessions, and leaving their PB&J sandwich remains on your homework. Your plans were often ruined when you had to babysit at the last minute.

## Firstborn Traits

1. perfectionist
2. achiever
3. leader
4. can be seen as bossy
5. responsible
6. motivated
7. conscientious
8. controlling
9. cautious
10. reliable

Because of your heightened responsibilities and perception of yourself as the family standard-bearer, you became very conscientious, reliable, capable, logical, and a list-maker. You are a black-and-white thinker with a keen sense of right and wrong. You believe there is a "right way" to do things. You feel like you always have to be right and perfect, or you'll let the adults in your life down. It's no wonder you've become a perfectionist.

Surprises are your enemy because you can't plan for them. You're often labeled a "Type A personality" because you're hardwired to succeed and plow ahead, no matter the difficulty of the circumstances or the height of the hurdles. You might be seen as aggressive, but you are always harder on yourself than you are on others. Or you might be seen as compliant, but inside you have a stubborn streak a mile long and a mile high. You're as immovable as a brick wall when you set your mind that something has to happen a certain way.

### The Only

You have likely felt and thought all the things that a firstborn does but x10 in intensity. After all, you are the *sole* standard-bearer in your family. Their entire reputation rests on you, so everything you do is observed, evaluated, and magnified. With no distraction of siblings, your parents' eagle eyes have been focused keenly on you since the time you were born or adopted. At times Mom or Dad might have been overprotective or overbearing, jumping to your aid before you asked for help.

Because you were surrounded by adults since birth, you found it difficult to identify with your peers. One look at that unruly bunch at the kindergarten door was enough to send you hightailing it back to the safety of Mom or Dad's legs. School was like entering another planet with no training. Those noisy peers didn't understand your need for quiet, order, and roadmaps. They seemed juvenile and silly since you were socialized with adults at home.

| Only Child Traits |
|---|
| 1. confident |
| 2. conscientious |
| 3. responsible |
| 4. perfectionist |
| 5. center of attention |
| 6. mature for their age |
| 7. seek approval |
| 8. sensitive |
| 9. a natural leader |

It's no wonder that you feel most comfortable even now with older adults. You act mature beyond your years. You were, in fact, a little adult by age seven or eight. You also love to work independently. You can't stand when others in your group drop the ball. You feel like you have to pick it up by default.

You crave alone time, where the world slows down and you have time to think. Your idea of a good day is a few minutes of sitting in the sunshine with a treasured book. But you are also the one most likely to set your cell-phone alarm so you can have that break time and still accomplish the rest of the 17 bullet points on your to-do list by the end of the day.

### The Middleborn

You often wondered as a child, *Will anyone notice if I go missing?*

You felt invisible, squished between Mr. Star and the little pipsqueak who got attention no matter what she did because she was "cute." When your siblings fought, you learned to keep your mouth shut, lay low, and watch the fireworks from a safe, hidden spot. If possible, you exited stage left until the fuss was over. You were adept at avoiding conflict. When you had to intervene, you played mediator because you wanted quiet in the house again. Even though you were good at seeing multiple sides of an issue and finding compromises, that didn't mean you liked being put in that position.

### Middleborn Traits

1. adaptable
2. independent
3. go-between
4. people-pleaser
5. can be rebellious
6. feels left out
7. peacemaker
8. social

Other family members didn't often ask you what you thought or how you felt. They couldn't have heard you anyway over the noisy baby. They were always busy attending the activities and honors of the firstborn. Sometimes you feel like an alien in your own family, with hardly any photos of you unless you were lodged like a prop between your siblings. That's why, to this day, friends are so important to you, and you're intensely loyal to your social group.

You also learned early to walk to the beat of a different drummer. You had no interest in competing with your firstborn sibling because you knew you couldn't win. Instead, you pursued your own path, which usually meant going the opposite direction of your older brother or sister. If he was a star athlete, you focused on music. If she was a math whiz, you wrote stories.

### The Lastborn

You were the little charmer, the fledgling in the family nest who got the most attention because you were always up to something. You're uncomplicated, spontaneous, humorous, and high on people skills. At home you played the role of entertainer... and also sacrificial lamb. When your siblings wanted something from Mom or Dad, whom did they send? You, the one most likely to accomplish the mission without getting killed. Besides, if you caught an earful for asking for something ridiculous, your sister thought, *It's about time. You deserve it.*

After all, you knew exactly how to get her in trouble. You were a natural-born manipulator. One touch, one scream like you'd been stabbed, and Mom came running like a trained dog to rescue her baby. You sometimes acted incapable so your older brother would do for you what you should do for yourself, like tying your shoes or packing your backpack. He did it out of self-protection. He knew it would get done faster that way so he could go about his business and wouldn't get blamed for work that wasn't done. That's also why he still treats you like a baby, and your sister continues to call you by your pet name.

| Lastborn Traits |
| --- |
| 1. social |
| 2. charming |
| 3. outgoing |
| 4. uncomplicated |
| 5. manipulative |
| 6. seeks attention |
| 7. self-centered |
| 8. focused on fun |

To this day, you love to meet people and have fun. You're the first person at work to suggest a group lunch or other social event. You've never met a stranger. You can befriend a rock. Yet even with those skills, people sometimes don't take you or your work seriously. That can be discouraging. It's easy to fulfill expectations when people don't have any of you.

## Work It Out

Reflect on the three siblings who experienced a childhood penny-pinching year.

1. *Sister #1:* Felt anxious, wondered if the family would be okay, and wished she could work to help out.

2. *Brother:* Wanted everyone to be happy and get along, disappeared when things got stressful, and missed having time with friends.

3. *Sister #2:* Remembered that year as a happy highlight of childhood, a time of family fun, and enjoyed being the center of attention.

Based on what you've learned about the birth orders, which one do you think is the firstborn? The middleborn? The lastborn? Why?

How might an only child reflect on that same childhood event?

Which birth order tugs most at your empathy? Why do you think that is?

Now that you've read about the birth orders, which traits in *your* birth order prompted you to say, "Wow, that's definitely me"? Which traits did you say, "That one's way off. I'm more like (name another birth order) in that regard"? The birth order traits I've listed above are *general* ones I've seen and identified in decades of counseling and consulting. As stated earlier, you are one-of-a-kind, influenced by a unique combination of variables.[7] For this book, understanding birth order is intended to help you *start* identifying areas you need to think about and work on in regard to leadership.

That's why we turn next to the strengths and weaknesses of each birth order.

## Strengths and Weaknesses of the Birth Orders

I once talked shop with a brilliant 20-something who's about as "Renaissance" as a human can get. Her interests and expertise already spanned so many areas that even entrepreneurs in their 50s couldn't dream of. Yet when I spoke to her of her natural skills, she brushed them off as ones that everybody had.

"No," I told her, "everybody cannot do that. You are unique in that skill combination."

Though she's an only child, she's certainly not alone in that kind of thinking. Oftentimes our strengths are those qualities so engrained in us that we don't think they're all that special. If that's you, it's time to recognize your strengths for what they are and learn how to take the best advantage of them.

On the flipside, when you can also recognize and assess weaknesses as inherent to your birth order, they no longer feel so…well, *personal.* They transform into easier-to-tackle issues that can be addressed proactively in bite-sized pieces. Such an approach helps you strategize next steps logically, without the emotional weight of guilt, failure, and frustration that often accompanies addressing areas that aren't your natural bent.

Every birth order has their strengths and weaknesses. Since firstborns and onlies have similar strengths and weaknesses, I'll group them when addressing some traits but also point out a few differences.

---

**LEMANISM #4**

Whatever your birth order, your greatest strengths are likely your greatest weaknesses.

---

### The Firstborn

I once spoke to a state society of accountants about birth order. As I looked out from the podium, exactly 221 people were staring at me with suspicion like I was about to waste their time or glancing at their phones for the next item on their to-do list. To loosen up the crowd, I said, "Will all of you firstborns and only children please rise?"

All but 19 got out of their chairs. To those 19, I asked, "What are you doing *here*?" The entire room roared with laughter, a feat difficult to accomplish with that typically controlled group. With the ice broken, I could get right to business on the topic at hand.

There's a reason firstborns and onlies are cautious, detailed, and no-nonsense and enter professions that require those traits. From the minute they started out in life, they've been figuratively wading into a lake with an unfamiliar bottom with eagle eyes watching their every move. No wonder they inch their way along, tentatively feeling with their toes for that drop-off they suspect could be only inches away. Both birth orders crave structure and roadmaps.

Firstborns come in two basic flavors: aggressive and compliant.

If you're the assertive, aggressive firstborn, leadership probably comes easily. Others appreciate your ability to take charge and know what to do. It's easy for you to command respect because you're used to getting it. You're known for your promise "I'll take care of it" and your ability to back up that statement. You are focused on your goals, driven, ambitious, enterprising, and energetic. You are willing to sacrifice to be a success, including putting in extra hours. You're also likely to be noticed because you're out in front of the pack.

But there's a downside to the aggressive firstborn. You may be so focused on your goals that you unwittingly run over others. You may not know how to show appreciation to others for their work because you are self-motivated. As a result, others may view you as insensitive, selfish, demanding, overbearing, or arrogant. If you're a workaholic, your drive and long hours puts your colleagues under a lot of pressure to match that pace.

That's why, if you find it difficult to get people to team up with you to do projects, you might want to reflect on how driven you are. If those who serve with you could tell you the truth, perhaps what they'd like to say is, "Lighten up!" or "Please slow down. I want to work with you. But I don't feel comfortable running that fast."

> Firstborns come in two basic flavors: aggressive and compliant.

If you're a compliant firstborn, it's because you're a perfectionist who views herself as failing, or having the potential to fail, in some arena. From Day One you were programmed for success by the all-powerful beings called *parents*. As your only role models, they seemed to know everything and held you to a high standard. Their eagle eyes were fixated on you. As a result, you avoided failure like the plague, because you could not accept it as an option. When their high standard became impossible for you to meet and your decisions were made *for* you instead of *by* you, the negative effects of critical-eyed perfectionism began to influence your thoughts and actions.

Here's how that critical eye played out in Loren's life. At a young age, he happily made his bed for the first time and proudly showed off his accomplishment to his mom. "Oh, that's nice, honey," she said as she smoothed out a wrinkle and adjusted a corner tuck. Later, he noticed that Mom had remade his bed. That same week Dad "helped" with the science project that Loren had already completed. What did Loren learn? That nothing he could do would ever be good enough, so why try? He'd only fail to be perfect.

With critical-eyed, perfectionistic parents, is it any wonder that firstborns have a high bar when it comes to performance? The apple doesn't fall far from the tree. Such colleagues tend to be detailed and critical. They can pick out a flaw from 40 yards away, are never satisfied when a job is completed, and always find something more that should have been done.

Their colleagues get off easy, though, compared to the firstborns, who hold themselves to an even higher standard. For perfectionists, life is never perfect. Friedrich Nietzsche's infamous statement speaks in painful volumes: "The worst enemy you can meet will always be yourself." Firstborns tend to beat themselves up emotionally when they cannot attain perfection. Anything other than meeting that high bar, they view as a failure. As such, they can tend to procrastinate.

Think about it. If you believed a project had to be perfect or it would be a failure, would you jump right in to do it? Or would you put it off…then put it off again? Why? Because you fear you can't do it well enough.

> For perfectionists, life is never perfect.

Whenever I counsel a client who struggles with perfectionism, the first thing we talk about is his parents and their expectations. In most cases, that client has been set up to be a perfectionist by a critical-eyed parent. In some cases, it's been *two* critical-eyed parents, like what happened to Loren. It's no surprise that later in childhood he avoided failure by acquiescing to his parents' wishes in all things. To keep the waters of life smooth at home and not induce a tsunami, he followed his father into the same career. Later, in that career he hated, he avoided failure by procrastinating and passing the buck to others until upper management noticed. That's when he arrived in my office.

---

**LEMANISM #5**

If you're a firstborn or only, flaunt your imperfections.
Try making a few mistakes. Risk a little.
Believe it or not, life will go on.

---

### The Only

Only children are super firstborns. The same traits of firstborns apply to onlies but are magnified. You are prepared and organized, hardworking, perfectionistic, and may be viewed as bossy and aggressive because you are so intently focused on your goals.

If you're an only child, the important question is *why* you were an only. The two basic possibilities are these:

1. Your parents planned to have only one child, whether through birth or adoption, and stuck with the plan. Typically that means your upbringing was tightly structured and highly disciplined. You were pressed to be responsible, dependable, and a grown-up.

2. Your parents could only have one child, whether through birth or adoption, so all their energy and attention got poured into you, the special jewel in the family crown. You were the center of their universe as you grew up. A certain amount of feeling special and spoiling came along with the bargain. As a result, you might also have some strong lastborn traits since the world seemed to revolve around you.

How do those possibilities play out?

Many only children who grew up with possibility #1 often appear cool, calm, and unreadable on the surface. I know because I've counseled many of them and their parents. That unruffled exterior is a protective measure. Such children are perfectionists who don't want to be known for who they truly are because then they might be rejected or fail at what really matters to them. Appearing in control on the outside keeps all the balls on their side of the court, so no one knows what they really think and feel.

Underneath, though, they may seethe with inner rebellion. They resent having to be little adults always on display for their parents. They are never given the opportunity to make their own decisions. Even choices such as what clothes they will wear, what friends they can have, what instrument they will play, what sport they are involved in, and what foods they will eat are made for them on a daily basis to protect the family's reputation.

Yes, such children may play by the parental rules during their teen and college years, when the parental units are still paying the bills. However, when such onlies reach adulthood, they tend to kick off any shackles binding them. That includes leaving relationships in the dust and completely switching careers. No surprise there for me as a psychologist. Would you want to live a path that someone else planned out for you? Yet such moves often mystify parents who have been in the driver's seat for their child's entire life.

Onlies who have grown up with possibility #2 are often sheltered and cushioned from the hard realities of

> Only children are
> super firstborns.

life in their earlier years. Since they are the center of the universe, they understandably may develop a trait of feeling overly important. To their benefit and detriment, they get all the parental attention. They don't have to share with siblings.

Problem is, when onlies venture into the world, things sometimes don't go the way they expect. Other birth orders think, *Well, that happens sometimes,* and go on with life unfazed. But onlies can be tempted to think they're being treated unfairly.

It's no surprise, then, that only children often get slapped with the labels *spoiled, selfish, lazy, aloof,* and *lonely.* But such is not necessarily so. The well-adjusted only child who realizes that others are just as important in the universe often has great initiative, healthy self-worth, and doesn't feel all that lonely. If this is you, then the sky really is the only limit. I'll sit back in my easy chair, watch you take off, and fly....

## Strengths and Weaknesses of Firstborns and Onlies In Regard to Leadership

*Trait:* Leader

*Strengths:* Take charge, know what to do.

*Weaknesses:* May undermine the initiative of others who lean on them too much, or may come off as too overbearing.

*Trait:* Aggressive

*Strengths:* Command respect, unflinching leaders others want to follow.

*Weaknesses:* Can run over others, may be insensitive or selfish, too focused on the goal and not enough on the feelings of others.

*Trait:* Compliant

*Strengths:* Cooperative, easy to work with, good team player.

*Weaknesses:* Can be taken advantage of, bullied, bluffed.

*Trait:* Perfectionistic

*Strengths:* Always do things right, leave no stone unturned to do a thorough job.

*Weaknesses:* Tend to criticize themselves or others too much, are never satisfied, may procrastinate out of fear of failure.

*Trait:* Organized

*Strengths:* Have everything under control, tend to be on time and on schedule.

*Weaknesses:* Overly worry about order, process, and rules, may not be flexible when it's needed, can be impatient with those they view as less meticulous, less competent, and less organized.

*Trait:* Driver

*Strengths:* Ambitious, enterprising, energetic, willing to sacrifice to be a success.

*Weaknesses:* Put too much stress and pressure on themselves and others.

*Trait:* List maker

*Strengths:* Set goals and reach them, tend to get more done in a day.

*Weaknesses:* May become boxed in, too busy with the to-do list to see the big picture of what needs to be done right now and what can wait until later.

*Trait:* Logical

*Strengths:* Known as straight thinkers, can be counted on not to be compulsive or to go off half-cocked.

*Weaknesses:* May believe they're always right, may fail to pay attention to the more intuitive opinions of others from which they and their work could benefit.

*Trait:* Scholarly

> *Strengths:* Tend to be voracious readers, accumulators of information and facts, good problem-solvers who think things through.
>
> *Weaknesses:* May spend too much time gathering facts instead of acting, may be so serious they fail to see the humor in situations.

Before we move to middleborns and lastborns, there are two things you need to know. First, if you're a firstborn or only, you can be awfully intimidating to the other birth orders. They not only think you walk on water, but they frequently see you doing that. Second, with all the attention and accolades firstborns and onlies get, laterborns often feel they're starting out life's race at a disadvantage. After all, the firstborns are already out there running strong.

Well, let me assure you that middleborns and lastborns have gifts that some firstborns would love to have. More often than not, entrepreneurs are middleborns. The best salespeople are lastborns. Being born later gives you an edge, especially with people. You're far more likely to be a good negotiator, mediator, and deal maker. You're also more likely to be skilled in reading people and knowing how to engage with them. Then there's the lastborn specialty—making people laugh.

Middleborns and lastborns were also relieved of that toughest-of-all jobs on earth: growing up firstborn. Laterborns didn't have to be the experimental guinea pig of parents who didn't quite know what they were doing but wanted their firstborn to do it right. Your firstborn sibling ran more interference for you than you know. Remember all those lectures he got that began with, "You're the oldest. I expected more out of you than that"?

Your firstborn sibling snow-plowed your roads of life, so say thank you sometime. He made it possible for you to be a kid. He became your role model. Because he was far less than perfect, you didn't inherit the same perfectionism he got from having Mom and Dad as his role model. You also didn't have to live with the pressure of believing the reputation of the family depended on you. You got away with a lot more than your firstborn sibling ever did. You didn't live with the weight of thinking, *If I don't do it, it'll never get done, and it'll be all my fault.*

So if you're a laterborn, you have a lot to celebrate. There are places for you as a leader that no firstborn can fill. Yes, you will have your strengths and weaknesses too, as we'll explore next. Everyone does. But don't think for a minute that being born later means you are born as less. It just ain't so….

> Being born later gives you an edge, especially with people. You're far more likely to be a good negotiator, mediator, and deal maker.

### The Middleborn

I live in Tucson, where we have a large quail population. Those birds are colored to blend into the desert in our backyard, so sometimes you can look right past them and not see them. But every once in a while, we get to watch a fascinating show: Mama Quail's industrious herding of her babies as they head off to the wild blue yonder.

The first baby is right in line, keeping right up with Mama's pace. The last baby tends to zigzag and get derailed until Daddy Quail appears out of nowhere and nudges him back into line. All those quail in the middle? They're the most unpredictable. But one thing's for sure. Usually the second quail in line isn't following the first one. She's doing her own thing.

Middle children are those not born first and not born last. They're the hardest birth order to analyze and the most unpredictable. That's because their style of operating has everything to do with two things that either work for them or against them.

First, if you were the child in the middle, you probably grew up feeling squeezed from above and below. You often went unnoticed. The star firstborn got all the attention because he did everything first, and he did it pretty well. The lastborn got attention because she forced others to pay attention to her with her antics. You didn't really *need* credit for things that you did, but sometimes it would have been nice to at least be acknowledged. That's why gathering your own group of people you liked and who liked you became very important.

Second, you were always playing off the firstborn above you. You couldn't do what he did as well as he did. Being a smart person, you reasoned, *Then why try? I'll do something completely different.* That's why, depending on what the firstborn is like, a middleborn can be a shy, quiet loner or a very friendly, team-player socialite. She might be the family rebel. He might play the role of peacemaker. She might appear easygoing because she wants to avoid conflict. He might be competitive and aggressive since it's the only way to seize attention.

## LEMANISM #6

If you're a middle child, look at the next older sibling to know what you *won't* be like.

You also may have developed an independent streak and a free spirit, even if it only showed itself internally for a while. If there were four children in your family and you were the third, the two siblings above you likely told you how to run your life. You learned how to nicely sidestep the advice you didn't want. You became the master of the art of give-and-take and compromise. You got used to intervening in sibling fights to carry messages to calm the waters.

You had no idea you were already in training, gaining and honing skills that would be invaluable for a career someday. Your ability to negotiate not only helps you get what you want but makes things better for those you serve and who serve with you. In business, winning friends and influencing people launches companies and helps them grow.

You're more comfortable with taking risks than a cautious firstborn. You're more capable of handling simultaneous details than the lastborn and don't crave the limelight. You listen well to others, can mediate well, and bring a deal to a successful conclusion. While lastborns excel at making sales, middleborns have the patience and staying power to make the deal and see it through. Middleborns are known for being independent thinkers who are willing to do things differently. They don't need accolades to keep on truckin'. That's why so many end up as entrepreneurs.

In short, middleborns, like firstborns and onlies, can be aggressive, compliant, or somewhere in the middle. But middleborns have a perk no other

> Middleborns are known for being independent thinkers who are willing to do things differently.

birth order has. You, above all others, know yourself a lot better already because you've seen life from a more realistic perspective. Nothing was ever easy for you. You weren't the firstborn star who could use his birthright to get his way. You couldn't get away with murder, like the lastborn manipulator in your family. You had to work for everything you got, so you don't shy away from hard work.

Like every birth order, though, your strengths are also your weaknesses. Middleborns are wise to learn well how to mitigate two specific weaknesses.

First, because you grew up wanting, needing, and searching out friends, relationships might be *too* important to you. Some middle children don't want to risk offending a colleague. Such a tug can cloud your judgment, prompting unwise decisions. If you and your colleagues are friends, can you still make a decision because it's the right thing to do, even if it makes one of them unhappy? If you cannot do that, you'll paint yourself into a tough corner someday. Perhaps it's a good time for a frank but kind conversation about friendship being friendship and work being work.

I know of two smart sisters who had that conversation prior to the middleborn starting work at the same company as the firstborn. As division leaders, they sometimes went head-to-head to solve problems. An hour later they'd eat lunch and plan weekend fun. They were so masterful at separating business and their personal relationship that none of their colleagues knew they were sisters until 10 years later, at the middleborn's bon-voyage party.

> Can you make a decision because it's the right thing to do, even if it makes a colleague temporarily unhappy?

Second, because you are good at working things out between people and have learned well the art of compromise, sometimes you are too compromising. You don't share your real feelings about a project, a decision, or perhaps a certain person in a key position who isn't upholding her share of the work. As a result, some may view your lack of sharing as the inability to analyze problems, to make decisions, or to be honest about issues. Others may see you as an easy target and move in like sharks that smell blood in the water to take advantage of you. If you're willing to have peace at any price, you'll be besieged with long work hours and have others steal credit for your projects. That's only for starters.

If there's one birth order that doesn't have to be told, "Life isn't fair," it's the middleborn. If you came through the trials of childhood in good shape, you've likely turned life's unfairness into strengths. You don't have unreasonable expectations like your firstborn sibling. You also don't have prince or princess syndrome like your youngest sibling. However, if your growing-up experience was rough, with those closest to you treating you poorly, you might be cynical, suspicious of others, rebellious, or bitter…all with good reason.

No matter who you are now, there's always room to grow. As one middleborn told me, "Although I hated being squashed in the middle as a kid, I see some real advantages to that position now that I'm an adult. I can cope with problems better than many of my colleagues. I got a lot of hands-on, beneficial training in give-and-take with my siblings. I learned that there will always be curveballs. If you stay calm and power on, you'll get the job done."

## Strengths and Weaknesses of Middleborns In Regard to Leadership

*Trait:* Reasonable expectations

> *Strengths:* Unspoiled and realistic since life hasn't always been fair.

> *Weaknesses:* May be suspicious, cynical, or bitter from being treated unfairly.

*Trait:* Social

> *Strengths:* Considers relationships as very important, is loyal, makes friends with colleagues easily and treats them like family.

> *Weaknesses:* Considers others as too important, and concern about offending them may cloud judgment on key decisions.

*Trait:* Independent thinker

*Strengths:* Willing to do things differently, take a risk, and strike out on your own.

*Weaknesses:* May appear to be bullheaded, stubborn, and unwilling to entertain others' ideas or cooperate on teamwork.

*Trait:* Compromising

*Strengths:* Know how to get along well with others and is skilled at mediating disputes and negotiating disagreements.

*Weaknesses:* Seen as willing to have peace at any price, and thus can easily be taken advantage of.

*Trait:* Diplomatic

*Strengths:* A peacemaker at heart, willing to go the second mile to work things out.

*Weaknesses:* Hate confrontation so choose not to share real thoughts, opinions, or feelings.

*Trait:* Secretive

*Strengths:* Can be trusted with sensitive information.

*Weaknesses:* Inability to admit when you need help.

---

### The Lastborn

Some years ago, the marmots, javelinas, and rats in Arizona converged on my car and chewed all the wires that counted to make the engine start. It was time to buy a new car. Friends recommended several options that had the kind of flash that usually attracts this baby of the family. But when it came to actually buying a vehicle, I did something else that comes naturally. I headed back to the dealership where I'd purchased my previous car and asked for the salesperson I'd dealt with before. That's because relationships are important to me.

When I walked into that showroom, I instantly spotted my dream car, a red convertible, sitting right out front. The salesperson approached a minute later. All I asked was, "That convertible in the front row…does it have leather seats and all the other goodies?"

I didn't ask for a sales brochure, a listing of the options, or a breakdown of the prices. I didn't ask how much the sales tax would be. I didn't say I'd weigh all the information and get back to him after a full evaluation if I wanted to proceed. All those are things that a firstborn would likely do.

No, this lastborn merely made two things clear. First, I wanted to buy that car and drive it home *today*. Second, as a person who cares about being economical, I would not pay more than $300 over invoice. The salesperson put up a bit of a fight on the second item but finally gave in, glimpsing a close-at-hand sale.

Fifteen minutes later, we had a deal. I didn't test-drive the car. I simply signed the papers and drove that car home. But as I took Sande, my firstborn wife, to the driveway to show off my new purchase, I suddenly began to have second thoughts.

To her credit, my supportive Sande cooed, "Oh, Leemie, I *love* it!"

Then, as I stood there smiling and proud of my taste in cars and my ability to get a good deal, Mama Bear brought me back to earth. "Except those chrome wheels *are* a *little* tacky," she emphasized.

I honestly hadn't noticed what color the wheels were. I was caught up in the thrill of the purchase. I share this story because it illustrates two key traits of lastborns. They are typically impulsive and impatient.

Contrast that to firstborns like my wife, who usually study a decision from every angle. They read the *Consumer Report* on every make and model they are considering, know the *Kelley Blue Book*® value of each, peruse every option and available accessory, and even research after-market costs of potential add-ons. They download vehicle manuals and read them cover to cover. They sleep on that choice for at least a week to ensure they don't miss an important aspect they should consider.

We won't even go into how long it takes my wife to research, decide on, and locate at nurseries the flowers she plants so artistically around our house every year. Nor how long it takes me to drive to the multiple places she flags in order to buy them. I do it happily for her because I love her and know how much it means to her. And boy, do those flowers look beautiful like Monet's garden reinvented every year.

But if it were only me as a lastborn on that mission, I'd simply head to the largest home-gardening store and hightail it to the plant section. A few minutes later, I'd have the flowers that caught my attention the most loaded up in the cart. No matter that they're for the wrong growing zone and are meant for shady rather than sunny areas.

You see, a lastborn always has places to go, people to see, and a purchase to show off. He can't be bothered with things like research. After all, time's a-wastin'!

> A lastborn always has places to go, people to see, and a purchase to show off. He can't be bothered with things like research.

Where does such impulsive impatience come from? As they grow up, lastborns are viewed as small and weak because they don't yet know how to do something. They live with low expectations because they're too little or too young to be taken seriously. Even if the adults in the family minimally expect a few

48

responsibilities, those babies can't escape the condescension that superior older siblings toss their way. Is it any wonder lastborns go through life muttering, "I'll show them!"? Such thinking prompts them to flit from area to area to find one where they can do just that.

They might play the role of Crown Prince or Princess in the spotlight. They might be viewed as cuddly, spoiled, and good for laughs. But, deep down, what lastborns really want is to be taken seriously. They often aren't sure exactly how they feel. One minute they might be at their charming, entertaining best. The next they'll be moody, rebellious, or even embarrassed by how they perceive that others view them.

What lastborns need most is to learn how to transform their weaknesses into strengths they can use in positive, productive ways to gain the attention and respect that they crave. Following are six ways lastborns can do that to their own and others' benefit.

First, you can be your naturally charming self without acting too "slick." We've all encountered salesperson types who drip so much charisma they seem oily enough to make us shudder and want to escape. Don't be that person. If you're a typical lastborn, you are likable, easy to talk

> Deep down, what lastborns really want is to be taken seriously.

to, and have a gift of keeping things around you interesting. Such qualities developed as you learned how to read the people around you. That includes those in your family, teachers and coaches at school, neighbors, and colleagues. Use that real skill to your and others' benefit without overplaying your card, and you'll fly high in life.

Second, you can be people-oriented without using chatting with others to escape responsibility. Many lastborns come across as undisciplined, too prone to talk and not work. Talking a good game but not being able to make it happen isn't a recipe for good relationships or career success.

As a lastborn, you already know you thrive in settings where you can relate to others, which potentially makes you a great team player. Why not mix and match your penchant for being comfortable in social settings with getting business done? Play a game of golf or tennis or have dinner at a fun restaurant with a client, and it's a win-win for you, your company, and that client. Or gather all the folks who've worked with you on a non-profit project for a friendly backyard barbecue where everybody brings their favorite dish and you provide the grill, the meat and veggie-friendly options, and the festive atmosphere.

Third, you can use your persistence to show the world what you can do in *positive* ways. I grew up as the clown in my family and continued that role in the classroom. Every teacher I had, except one, labeled me as the student most likely to fail. It wasn't until that one teacher told me I had skills, and I started dating the lovely woman who would become my wife, that I decided I'd never again consider myself a failure. I'd also never take the words, "No, you can't do that," as final. I'd simply see what I *could* do.

---

**LEMANISM #7**

If you're a lastborn, instead of trying hard to show *them,* show *yourself* what you can do.

---

Fourth, your ability to be spontaneous and uncompli-cated has its perks, and you know them well. You don't sweat preparing for events like a firstborn would. You show up and do your thing. These same qualities, though, can prompt others to view you as disorganized, absentminded, unfocused, or even airheaded. Doing some planning and preparing before an event won't kill you. It will help others see some of your good qualities.

Not only can you play well, but they can also count on you to get the job done.

Fifth, you are naturally self-confident due to your lastborn trait of wanting attention. All kids crave attention, but lastborns make a career out of it. Usually they try to get that attention by being funny. Such moves may prompt others to think you are all about yourself. Instead, save your unparalleled ability to get attention and entertain for when it counts and serves others. Then you'll earn yourself a spot at work and in your relationships that no one else has. Sometimes a tense meeting needs a bit of humor to get everyone to breathe and move onto the same page. Or a boring meeting requires a pep-up moment. You are the perfect person to step up on both occasions.

Sixth, your natural aptitude to engage well with others is an excellent quality for business and relationships. But it also needs to be balanced with taking time to think things through. You can't know or help the whole world, but you *can* influence a carefully chosen corner of it.

## Strengths and Weaknesses of Lastborns In Regard to Leadership

*Trait:* Charming

> *Strengths:* Easy to talk to, make events fun and interesting, and people like you.

> *Weaknesses:* Can come across as a little too slick or a bit unbelievable.

*Trait:* People-oriented

> *Strengths:* Excel relationally in both group and one-on-one settings.

> *Weaknesses:* May come across as undisciplined, too prone to talk and not work, unable to provide details, and able to talk a good game but not carry out or finish a job.

*Trait:* Persistent

> *Strengths:* Tireless in the pursuit of reaching goals, getting what you want, and won't take no for an answer.

> *Weaknesses:* Sometimes push too hard because you see things only your way.

*Trait:* Friendly and engaging

> *Strengths:* Reach out to others easily and engage with them in a friendly manner because you like such exchanges yourself.

> *Weaknesses:* Can be seen as too impulsive or emotional in making moves or decisions without giving them enough thought.

*Trait:* Uncomplicated

> *Strengths:* Appear genuine and trustworthy with no hidden agenda.

> *Weaknesses:* Can come off as ditzy or unfocused.

*Trait:* Attention-seeking

> *Strengths:* Know how to get noticed, typically by entertaining.

> *Weaknesses:* Can appear self-centered, unwilling to give others credit.

## Great Leaders at Their Best

Great leaders aren't perfect. They have lots of weaknesses. That's why, in the next chapter, we will explore leadership traits, how to develop and fine-tune them, and the important difference between being a *perfectionist* and being a *seeker of excellence.*

One is self-defeating, and the other will power you on to new heights you can't even imagine.

Great leaders choose to focus on their strengths and work to shore up their weaknesses. When one approach doesn't work, they re-strategize the battlefield and then attack the issue again, armed with past experience and new knowledge. That's why, after exploring the birth orders, it's time to pause and allow you to reflect on what you've learned.

## Work It Out

### Which Birth Order Are You?

Look at the traits, strengths, and weaknesses of your birth order.

Which strengths do you see in yourself? How might you use those to your best advantage in your arenas of influence (work, home, other)?

What weaknesses do you see in yourself? How might you address those weaknesses? Brainstorm ideas and put one into action this week.

What's your most important personal takeaway from learning about and assessing yourself in light of your birth order?

How do you operate the best? How will you use your strengths and shore up your weaknesses? What can you uniquely contribute as a leader?

One firstborn leader I know is a tricycle person by nature. He likes to go slow, examine every detail of a project, and run lots of scenarios before launching a product idea. So what does he do? He stays in the tricycle lane. He doesn't get on the expressway because driving in the fast lane is not his gift.

Instead, he focuses on his strength, which is new product development. Most days you'll find him in his khakis or jeans, hunkered down in front of assorted metal parts. Because these are years-down-the-pike concepts, he can spend time exploring every possibility. When the item does go into production, he knows all the kinks have already been worked out. He can feel good about the quality he is extending to his valued customers.

That leader, because he understands birth order, installed a fast-driving, efficient, and detailed firstborn Operations Manager to run his current product line. He also hired a middleborn Office Manager who is adept at juggling his and the Operations Manager's personalities, along with any questions and concerns of the product-line workers. With this line-up, that small company is now growing like wildfire. Ask any employee, and they'll tell you, "This is a great place to be. We get to do interesting work every day, and the owner and managers listen and care about us."

### Thoughts of a Successful Leader

Concentrate on your strengths,
instead of your weaknesses...
on your powers,
instead of your problems.

PAUL J. MEYER, AMERICAN BUSINESSMAN

Another leader I know is a lastborn entrepreneur. Her ability to relate to people and share the vision of her nonprofit through social media led to it skyrocketing in its first year. Then the problems started. Soon she had more meetings than she could keep up with, and the tedium of details weighed her down and dampened her enthusiasm.

Then she discovered birth order. She realized she wasn't the organized, detailed type, never would be, and didn't have to be. She could happily be that charming lastborn who encouraged others to join her in making the difference she longed to make. With a smile, she hired a trustworthy firstborn known in the field for being laser-focused on details, including growing nonprofits in sustainable ways.

Then she trusted that firstborn to hire an onlyborn accountant and a middleborn to manage the owner's social media campaign and accompany her to social gatherings. Those four women are rocking and rolling on that company. Each is so different, but the strategy works. No one steps on any other's toes because they all have their areas of expertise.

That, my friends, is how you can use birth order to your best advantage and to the advantage of all those you serve with.

## Winning Play #2
## Grow Your Leadership Traits

*Promote active engagement*
*by balancing healthy authority*
*and support with high expectations*

I once observed a fledgling group violin teacher attempting to herd all her little ducklings into a line. She wanted them to practice moving onto the stage for an upcoming concert. But here's the problem.

Those little ducklings did not want to listen, nor did they desire to be herded. They wanted to do their own thing. The noise that ensued was deafening, and chaos reigned, threatening the delicate instruments.

The teacher, finally at her wits' end, shouted at the top of her voice, "I'm the leader! And you need to do what I say right now!"

That outburst prompted no change in student behavior. It took a veteran teacher, schooled in the art of managing children, to begin quietly moving the student leaders into line. Those student leaders then corralled the violin players in their charge into line behind them.

A few minutes later, order reigned. The students were silent and attentive. The practice could go on.

That young teacher learned a hard lesson that day. If you have to say, "I'm the leader," you're not. Sure, you might be the assigned leader and think you're the highest on the totem pole for the day, but that doesn't mean others will view you as a leader.

## What Leaders Are...and Are Not

Many people think that the loudest, most dominant person in the room is naturally the leader. Leaders, to them, are always outspoken, charismatic, and forceful. But that's not true.

> If you have to say, "I'm the leader," you're not.

In fact, here's a secret you should know. Often the loudest people are loud because they are insecure. They aren't confident of their place in the world, much less their leadership skills. They don't think they can get attention if they're not forcing people to pay attention to them.

Leadership doesn't come in only one package. It comes in all shapes, sizes, and types. Some of the most powerful leaders I know have been quiet, unpretentious, straightforward people who emerged as leaders because they were excellent at their craft, spoke up or acted when others couldn't make decisions, and were able to get a project on track and completed.

Take Lyra, a college sophomore who was at first treated like a fish out of water in a junior-senior project discussion. However, she had leadership skills. She was organized, highly focused, and tenacious. She instinctively knew how to read a room and how to get the best out of people. She did not push any agenda. She simply got busy doing what needed to be done. When there was a mountain to climb, she hated wasting valuable time.

So, while the older students socialized, Lyra got to work. She headed to a classroom whiteboard and started outlining potential categories and ideas. Five minutes later, one of her chatting peers noticed the developing board. He pointed at it and nudged a nearby colleague.

> Leadership doesn't come in only one package. It comes in all shapes, sizes, and types.

Soon all the juniors and seniors swiveled toward that board. Talking stopped. They stared at the board and then at Lyra, who was still working.

"Those are great ideas," one of the seniors said. "I especially like the one where…"

The students nodded as a group.

A senior the others clearly treated as top dog chimed in. "I agree. But how could we turn that idea into a workable project?"

Lyra turned to face the group and smiled. "It's simple…."

Ten minutes later, their project was in full swing, with bullet points noted by Lyra on that whiteboard, and each member heading a specific point. That group went from a disorganized mess to a well-run machine in half an hour. All it took was a person with leadership traits who decided to take a risk among her peers to become a positive force.

Would you be surprised if I told you that Lyra headed up every monthly meeting for the rest of the school year? And that the college marketed the results of that project as an example of how a student-backed group could influence their community for the good? Or that Lyra continued to use her leadership skills to launch or reinvigorate other groups on campus?

As a peer said a year later, "When Lyra steps into the room, everybody treats her like the leader. She has such a strong *presence* that you can't help but follow her and be energized. She's a team player who knows how to use every member's best skills, and she treats everyone equally with kindness and respect. No matter how crazy or busy it gets, she stays calm. We feel really good when we complete the project and look back at what we accomplished."

Sounds like a good recipe for a leader, doesn't it? A *leader* is, simply stated, *a person whom others will follow.* However, to those like Lyra, leadership isn't really about being the one in charge. It's about being a conduit for others' beneficial development, so that the group can feel good about their contributions and the completed project.

What's your definition of leadership? Good ol' *Merriam-Webster's Dictionary* defines leadership as "the office or position of a leader," "capacity to lead," and "the act or instance of leading."[8] That definition isn't very helpful, is it? It only highlights the *position* or *function* of a leader, not the *types* or *qualities* of a leader.

> Leadership isn't really about being the one in charge. It's about being the conduit for others' beneficial development.

## Work It Out

Take a few minutes to reflect on these questions:

1. Why did you decide to pursue leadership?
2. What factors played into that decision?
3. How would you define *leadership?*

Be assured these questions have no right or wrong answers. No one will answer those questions in exactly the same way. That's because leadership is, above all, *personal.*

That's why, in this chapter, we'll look first at the three types of leaders. We'll explore what healthy leadership looks like and how you can stay in the driver's seat with authority, while supporting your colleagues and getting the job done. It has everything to do with the healthy traits of a leader. You might be surprised how many you already have but didn't realize were leadership traits. Others may be a bit rusty in practice and need some polishing to make them shine. Still others may be new to you but will be of great benefit. Finally, we'll look at what "success" means in light of your intended legacy.

## Three Types of Leaders

If you're a leader-in-training, you are in a treasured spot. You get to choose right out of the gate the kind of leader you'd like to be. If you're already in leadership, you also have a choice. You can keep doing what you're doing, or you can consider an option that might be healthier for you in the long run and more beneficial for those you serve and who serve with you.

Leaders can be grouped into three styles depending on how they use authority. That style shapes how colleagues and clients respond. As you read the following descriptions, ask yourself, *Which leadership style sounds most like me right now? Which style sounds like one I'd like to work toward?* Remember, this book is about starting where you are on a Monday and working your way to becoming a great leader by Friday. A learning-for-a-lifetime attitude will take you far.

### The Authoritarian Leader

Picture a starkly decorated room in blues and grays. Identical cubicles are lined up in precise rows. Robot-like humans occupy the desks and do what they are told when they are told. There is no room for individuality or creativity. No opportunity to ask questions or give input. The goal for these workers is simply to complete their tasks so they can go home and do what they want to do.

Several times a day the leader walks the aisles to ensure everyone is doing what he expects. If they aren't, the verbal hammer comes down. "You are not paid to think or ask questions. You are paid to do what I say. Get to it." Punishment is meted out in front of the group with threats that anyone else who acts up will meet the same fate. "If this happens again," the leader stresses, "*all* of you will be held responsible. Test me, and you'll regret it."

Nobody wants to be the subject of the leader's wrath. That's why the majority of the robots do what they are told. However deep resentment flows like a never-ending river.

This description sounds like a futuristic movie, doesn't it? But, sadly, that's what life is like in an authoritarian environment. Authoritarians not only need to be in charge but to be *recognized* as the one in charge. That's why they tend to bark out orders. They like to tell colleagues how to do their jobs, rather than bring them along for the journey. They often view themselves as better than their colleagues due to their position.

An authoritarian has an intense need to be right. And, to follow that logic, if he is right, everyone else is wrong. His mantra is, "It's my way or the highway." There is no gray area, no in-between landing spot for anyone else.

He is the one who decides what things should be done, how they should be done, and when they should be done. Everything is about him, not the team. He makes all decisions without asking for or considering input from others. If something goes wrong, he is swift to lay the blame at a colleague's feet. If something goes right, he claims the credit.

> The Authoritarian Leader
> "It's my way or the highway."

For an authoritarian, life is streamlined. He doesn't have to involve others, since he's a one-stop shop. He doesn't have to field questions or consider other routes. However, not giving others the opportunity to voice ideas and questions means he may be shortsighted or miss the mark entirely on a project. One person cannot strategize every aspect. He wouldn't be human if he didn't miss something.

What about his colleagues? They have no freedom due to their leader's controlling style. There is no wiggle room to learn anything new. No opportunity to excel in their own right. No chance they will be recognized. Let me ask you: If you were on that team, would you stay? Or hightail it out that door as soon as you found another job opportunity? It's no wonder that the biggest concern of many authoritarian leaders is revolving-door syndrome.

Why do authoritarians approach leadership the way they do? Many were reared in a highly controlling environment with an authoritarian parent who was emotionally or physically unavailable but laid on the edicts when he was around. Parents reigned supreme and were never wrong. Children were "lesser than" humans who were supposed to do what they were told without question. Their every path and decision was made for them by an almighty parent who knew what was best.

Some children of authoritarian parents acquiesced out of fear. Others did so simply because it was easier than fighting the inevitable and getting grounded every week. Still others towed the line at home with a seemingly unruffled attitude but then became a different person when they were among their peers.

Each of those children vowed, *When I'm in charge, I will never, ever be like dear ol' dad. I'll never say what he did. I'll never do what he did.* Then, years later, they discover they not only say what he did but with the same inflection and a louder volume. They are doing what they used to hate.

Granted, change is never easy. In fact, it can be uncomfortable and a little threatening. It takes peeling away layers to find the issues and the root causes for a behavior. When you do, the turning-on-the-light-bulb moment comes.

For authoritarians, the issue is *control.* They have to be in control. In fact, they only count in this world when they are in control and can exert that control over others.

However, the root cause of that control is *fear.* They think, *If I can't control this situation and the outcome of this project, everything will go haywire. It'll be my fault. The project will be a failure. I'll be a failure. And the whole world will see that I'm a loser.*

You see, authoritarians are perfectionists. They cannot lose because failure is not only unacceptable but unthinkable. So if they are one percent behind their sales goal for the day, they cannot see the 99 percent win. They can only see the one percent failure. No wonder authoritarians try so hard to control processes and people. There is no margin for error.

Can you imagine living under that kind of pressure every day? If that's you, you don't have to live with it any longer, and you shouldn't. No one can perfectly hit the high bar every time they perform. There is a better way— the Leman Way. I guarantee it will be healthier for you and for all those you serve and who serve with you. By the end of this chapter, you'll be well on your way to freedom.

> Authoritarians are perfectionists. They cannot lose because failure is not only unacceptable but unthinkable.

### The Permissive Leader

Picture a lush green field with white and yellow daisies waving in the breeze under a blue sky with fluffy clouds. People skip through their day doing exactly what they want to. Prepared food and a blanket are provided for a picnic lunch. All they have to do is roll out that blanket, sit on it, and enjoy the food.

When lunch comes, those people whine and complain that they're tired. Putting out the blanket and the food is too much work. One person rises to the challenge. She says, "Oh, that's all right. I'm sure it's been a long morning for you. I'll take care of it. Is there anything else I can do for you?" By the way, she's the one who was up at 4:00 a.m. making that food and transporting it to that daisy field. The others didn't arrive until 8:00 a.m.

> **The Permissive Leader**
> "Is there anything else I can do for you?"

To keep the day going as planned and to ensure everyone stays relaxed, she lays out the blanket and the food herself. As the others eat, she watches with a smile. She basks in the enjoyment of them eating what she made. When her colleagues take a nap in the early afternoon sun to rest from their lackadaisical exertions, she quietly cleans up the mess. She tiptoes so she doesn't disturb them.

Later, when they are skipping through the daisies again, she thinks, *Ah, life is going well. Everybody is happy and having a good time.*

Such is the unrealistic world created under a permissive leader. Anything goes. Any "rule" can be bent or broken if it's inconvenient or upsets a colleague. Nothing in that environment is certain because it can always change. By putting the highest priority on everyone getting along and having a good time, that leader enables detrimental behavior.

Don't feel like completing that project? No problem, you don't have to.

Say something harsh to a client and lose them? Well, it's not your fault.

Here's the truth. No one can be happy and having a good time all the time. That's not real life. Trying to remove others' road bumps only leads to entitlement. And entitled people don't function well as a community to advance your directives.

A permissive leader does things for her colleagues that they should do for themselves. She finds it hard to say no to requests. If a colleague complains about a procedure, she changes it.

In short, a permissive leader is like a hamster running on a wheel. Once she starts capitulating to demands, she'll never be able to get off that wheel. Those colleagues have her figured out. Throw in a compliment once in a while, and she'll keep running in circles toward the elusive prize of making everyone happy.

Who is really in charge? The intended leader? No, it's one of the pack. And in pack behavior, the person in charge is typically the one who rises to top dog for the day. That constant fluctuation leads to an extremely chaotic environment.

> A permissive leader is like a hamster running endlessly on a wheel. Once she starts capitulating to demands, she'll never be able to get off that wheel.

Why would a leader allow such an environment? It's simple. Approval is paramount to her. She wants to be everyone's friend. She wants everyone to like her. That's why instead of laying down the law when it's needed, she will waffle on decisions that matter, lengthening the stress. She will attempt to cajole or bribe her colleagues with rewards if they do what she asks. None of those is a good way to fly as a leader.

Permissive leaders are well-intentioned. However, they rob their colleagues of self-respect by doing too much for them. Self-worth grows when you work hard to do a job well. At the end of the day you smile and think, *Look at that. I did that, and it feels really good. Boy, am I going to sleep well tonight.*

Permissive leaders also short-circuit the opportunity for learning by rescuing colleagues from natural consequences or, worse, taking away the need for a decision. Providing a Disneyland work experience inhibits a person's ability to perform in the long run. Inconsistent authority leads to too much freedom and too few guidelines and boundaries. It invites rebellion among the ranks. Colleagues can't trust the leader to adhere to any plans or deadlines or to back up what she says with action.

It would seem at first that permissive leaders are on the opposite end of the spectrum from authoritarian leaders. They are if you simply look at their actions and the way they carry them out. Permissive leaders want everybody to get along and bend over backwards to do whatever that takes. Authoritarians insist that others do things their way and when they say.

However, both styles have the same core issue: *control*. Both want to control the people and the situation. They simply carry out that control in different ways. Both also have *fear* as their root cause. While the authoritarian fears failure and being seen as a failure, the permissive leader fears that people won't like her.

Why is approval so important to a permissive leader? Her worth stems from the unrealistic idea that, to be worth something, everyone must like you at all times. That's a stressful way to live. No one will like you all the time. Some people won't like you some of the time. And other people? Well, they won't like you at all. That's life.

But there is a better, easier, and less stressful way to live.

### The Authoritative Leader

Picture a well-run workplace that is organized with its goals and individual colleagues in mind. Specific departments are uniquely arranged to assist the purpose of their work. The colleagues have given their own spins to their offices and desks. A walk-by makes you smile. You learn so much about the people, their hobbies, and what matters most to them. Observing the differences gives you something to talk about.

When colleagues arrive, they greet each other with friendly banter while pouring a mug of coffee or tea. Five minutes later, they are plunged into their work because they are excited about their projects and invested in them. Break times and lunches are filled with lively energy, camaraderie, the exchanging of ideas, and laughter. Colleagues listen to each other, problem-solve together, and respect each other.

> ## The Authoritative Leader
> "I trust you, respect you, and appreciate your work.
> I will support you, encourage you, and have your back."

Their leader is, above all, a role model. He lives out his mantra, "I trust you, respect you, and appreciate your work. I will support you, encourage you, and have your back." He is honest, trustworthy, responsible, hard-working, goal-oriented, prepared, and organized. He's a team player. He works to ensure that the vision of the company is front and center and that goals and deadlines of projects are posted where all have equal access. He regularly communicates with his colleagues individually and as a group.

He considers each of his colleagues as equals and treats them as such. He is not "better than" since he's the boss. His roles and responsibilities are simply different. He goes out of his way to connect with each colleague, showing that he cares about them personally. As a result, he knows them well and can place them in roles that align with their skills. All understand how their work impacts the overall vision of the company. They feel appreciated and valued.

An authoritative leader stays in healthy authority with high expectations and high support. He has a service-oriented, team-focused attitude and lives out the virtues and values he believes in. He pulls his own weight, doing what he says he will do, when he says he'll do it.

Who *wouldn't* want to work with such a leader? He creates a win-win environment for all. He establishes a middle ground between the extremes of authoritarianism ("my way or the highway") and permissiveness ("I'll do it for you, you poor,

> An authoritative leader stays in healthy authority with high expectations and high support.
> He has a service-oriented, team-focused attitude and lives out the virtues and values he believes in.

overworked dear"). He avoids prompting resentment and rebellion, assists in growing his colleagues' skills and bettering them as people, and allows them personal choices. Instead of forcing them to obey the rules, the authoritative leader *wins* their cooperation.

But how does he do it?

## What Healthy Leadership Looks Like

You have a project coming up that you know won't be a favorite. How might each of the leadership styles handle it?

The authoritarian leader would announce, "Here's the project. Check the board for the details and assignments. I'll expect it on my desk first thing tomorrow morning. If you have to work all night, so be it. That's the job." And he'd exit stage left.

The permissive leader would say, "This isn't a fun project, is it? Well, on second thought, don't worry about it. I'll stay late and do it myself tonight."

The authoritative leader would assemble the group, explain the project, goals, and intended outcomes. Then he'd say, "This project wouldn't be anyone's choice, would it?" He'd laugh, and that laughter would spread across the room. "But it's also part of our business, and each of you has a significant role in that business doing well. So let's knock it out together, as swiftly as possible and to the best of our abilities like we always do."

He'd promptly assign parts of the project to different colleagues to tackle. He'd let them know he is available for questions or brainstorming. Because their work culture is a "roll up your sleeves and help" one, they know he will dive in to help if they need it.

What happens next? The colleagues get right to work. They're invested in the community's welfare and know that the leader assigned portions of the project because he knows they will excel at them. They work seamlessly as a group, checking in with each other and their leader as needed to speed the project ahead.

By the end of the day, the project is done. The leader high-fives each colleague and then tells the group, "Thanks to each of you for your hard work today." He smiles. "I knew we could do it. Won't it feel great to walk out that door and have that behind us? I appreciate each one of you." All walk out the door that night smiling and satisfied with their work and their performance.

How can the authoritative leader be so different? That leader majors on relationships and minors on everything else. He doesn't have to prove he's in charge, because they already view him with respect and naturally follow him. He doesn't have to provide a Disneyland experience because they already like their work and want to do it. Who wouldn't? They are at a workplace where their leader respects them, encourages them, works with them, and even provides some fun and a surprise round of coffee to spur them on every once in a while.

You see, being a leader is all about connections. If you don't have a connection, why would your colleagues care what you ask them to do? Rules never work without first having a relationship. Your colleagues need to know they are part of a team. *Your* team. Sometimes you all succeed. Sometimes you fail. But you do it together and learn together.

---

**LEMANISM #8**

Healthy leadership starts with the 3 Rs.
Relationship. Relationship. Relationship.

---

## The 6 Traits of a Healthy Leader

How can you stay in the driver's seat with healthy authority that motivates your colleagues, supports your colleagues, *and* gets the job done? Leadership in any arena is not only doable but doable in a great way if you are equipped with practical no-nonsense information, a generous dose of motivation, and both short-term and long-term strategies. The following traits of a leader are imperative to accomplishing your goal.

### #1: Set and stick to your vision and goals.

A great leader always has his vision and goals in mind. He establishes a roadmap with signposts and uses them to measure the group's progress. He isn't afraid to take a brief respite to re-evaluate the plan if facts show that he should. But even if he decides to rearrange the route, he keeps his focus on his destination and doesn't give up until he gets there.

To make progress toward those goals, he knows he must be prepared and organized. Whatever he does on the front end to inform, motivate, and support his colleagues helps the work go much more smoothly. Organization extends to how he schedules his time, the materials he crafts and makes available, and the arrangement of the workspace.

### Work It Out

#### Top 5 Tips for Meetings

1. To respect participants' time and attention spans, structure meetings to be purposeful and no more than 20 minutes.

2. Prepare and distribute the agenda a day prior. Allot specific windows for each speaker to encourage a tight focus on any information shared.

3. Move to each agenda item at the scheduled time to accomplish the overall purposes of the meeting.

4. Assign items requiring more attention to a work group, who can report the highlights in a future meeting.

5. Thank all who participated for their information, brainstorming, and attention.

When a leader knows where he's going, sets up a workable structure, and details steps to get to a set destination, colleagues have a sense of security and stability. They are well-informed. They are supported by well-established routines and a leader who is not changeable like the wind.

Yes, it takes a lot of intentionality, purpose, direction, and clarity to create such an environment. But I promise you it's worth it. We'll talk about how to do that in Friday's chapter.

### #2: Role-model what is most important.

What are the core values and beliefs that matter most to you? The virtues you strive to live by? Do you talk about them and model them in every arena you inhabit?

If you want others to have integrity, you have integrity…even when your emotions want to take you in a different direction.

If you want others to work hard and take pride in their work, you work hard and always do your best.

### Thoughts of a Successful Leader

The most effective way to do it is to do it.

AMELIA EARHART, AMERICAN AVIATION PIONEER

If you want others to value time with family, then you prioritize family. You are present at the dinner table. You ensure that your colleagues can leave on time so they can be at their kids' baseball games and concerts.

If you want others to listen attentively, you listen attentively.

If you want others to give you the benefit of the doubt and hear the facts first before judging, you also do that in situations that inevitably crop up when human beings work together.

If you want others to be respectful and kind, you be respectful and kind.

In short, you cannot hold others to a standard that you yourself don't fulfill.

## Work It Out

1. Write a "Top 10 Priorities" list of what is most important to you.

2. Skim that list every morning for the next week.

3. At the end of the week evaluate decisions you've made and the hours you've spent in light of that list. Where have you met or exceeded that list? Which areas need a bit more attention the following week?

### #3: Respect, trust, support, and appreciate your colleagues.

Respect is a two-way street and a critical foundation for any work. Great leaders know the difference between a bridle and a bit. That's why they provide standards and parameters but allow flexibility and freedom. They are confident their team can rise to any challenge.

When considering projects, great leaders evaluate their goals, the facts of a project, and solicit input from their team. They value that input due to their colleagues' unique skills and varying perspectives. Once that information is gathered, that leader decides how the project will be run because that is one of his roles. He plans the next steps, details them for his team, and then trusts each of them to do what they do best.

But the great leader doesn't stop there. He also supports his team members. He is their advocate, listening ear, and a lifeline when they need it. He offers assistance but doesn't force it. He exercises patience and waits for them to ask for help since that is respectful of them.

He also states and shows his appreciation for each colleague. To him, differences aren't threatening. They are invigorating and empowering. He knows that together they can do it better than he could ever do it alone.

Saying "thank you" and "I appreciate you" in today's culture is rare. Don't let it go extinct. All it takes is a few seconds to make a little comment to showcase your appreciation. Colleagues not only respect but want to please an appreciative leader. Courtesy never goes out of style.

### #4: Expect the best.

Want to unleash your colleagues' potential and motivate them toward success as well as ramp up the success of your company? Then expect the best and you're more than likely to get the best. People respond far better to carrots than they do sticks.

> Colleagues not only respect but want to please an appreciative leader.

If you say, "We need to hit this month's sales goals. If we don't, we might have to look at some layoffs," you introduce fear and competition. Add to that a round of backstabbing from colleagues who try to one-up each other so they don't lose their jobs. Threatening or punishing *does* work, but not in the way you might think. Such actions prime colleagues to rebel.

Great expectations with a dose of reality can make a great difference. When you say, "Okay, folks, the sales goal this month is X. Yes, it's higher than usual because we need to make up for last month's shortfall. But I believe in you. I know you'll get the job done."

You smile. "As an extra perk, I've decided that when we meet our goal this Friday, we'll have an early lunch on the company. It'll be one of five places decided by your vote. I'll post the places right after this meeting. Even better, you'll get the rest of the afternoon off to spend however you want. I hope you, your friends, and families will enjoy it."

What have you done? You've set the rules for the scenario. A+B=C.

A. The colleagues work hard.
+B. They accomplish their goal.
=C. Free lunch and the afternoon off.

Note that the freebie lunch and time off are contingent on hard work and making that sales goal. If the goal isn't made, natural consequences follow. There is no lunch. No time off. Both your expectations and the results are clear-cut.

If A+B happens, then C follows.

If A+B doesn't happen, then no C follows.

It's a simple formula that doesn't change. This method only works, though, if you mean what you say and you stick to the plan with no waffling or giving in. When colleagues know you mean business, trust and respect flourish.

### Thoughts of a Successful Leader

High achievement always takes place
in the framework of high expectations.

CHARLES KETTERING, AMERICAN INVENTOR
AND ENGINEER

One last thing. When you set your standards of performance, make sure they are attainable. If they aren't, those who serve with you will become discouraged and give up. They won't rise to any challenge, and they certainly won't have good thoughts and feelings toward you.

Have you ever met the standards you expect of your colleagues? Are they realistic? Set the bar high, yes. But make it attainable. After all, you're on the hook too. The higher the bar, the more support you need to give your colleagues.

### #5: Make tough decisions when needed.

Great leaders make a lot of decisions, and not all of them are easy. They are ultimately responsible for the work and the people onboard. That means paying careful attention to everything from hiring to minimizing friction and optimizing solutions to the horrible job of firing when absolutely necessary.

> The higher the bar, the more support you need to give your colleagues.

Who you choose to surround yourself with will say a lot about you and directly impact the success of your venture. Yes, it takes all kinds to make the world go 'round. However, some people will be more challenging to your end goals.

I always tell CEOs, "Hire personality. You can teach people what they need to know to do their job well. But you cannot reshape their personality." That's why you should never trust the facts on a résumé 100 percent. Neither should you accept letters of recommendation at face value. That résumé deserves more than a 30-second skim as it crosses your desk.

### Thoughts of a Successful Leader

Trust, but verify.

RONALD REAGAN, 40TH PRESIDENT OF THE UNITED STATES,
MANTRA FROM THE COLD WAR DAYS

You should review it carefully and then dig for the facts yourself. Meet that person face-to-face for an interview. Throw in a curveball or two and see how he responds. Try, "If you could design a perfect day, what would it look like?" What he says and how he says it will reveal a lot about his personality and how it might mesh or clash with others already on staff.

> Hire personality. You can teach people what they need to know to do their job well. But you cannot reshape their personality.

There's another reason for a careful review. Many a CEO has told me, "When I saw that person's résumé, I never would have hired her. I didn't think she had enough experience. But I'm so glad I decided to give her a shot. She's been with us for only six months, and she's already a star performer. People she works with only say good things about her. My bet? She'll help us start a new division in about two or three years."

Every leader faces that quandary when a colleague cannot do the work he's assigned to do. *Fun* would not be the top descriptor in anyone's assessment of that situation. Even the toughest veteran leaders hate to fire people. However, when you're responsible for a company or project, that role sometimes requires difficult conversations.

When a great leader has to let someone go, she does it with respect, kindness, and care. She is straightforward, focusing not on the person as incompetent but on the job responsibilities. "Thank you for taking time to meet with me. I wanted to talk with you about your job responsibilities. The position you're currently in requires specific skills and traits." She lists them. "On the last three projects, your work does not showcase such skills or traits as your natural fortes. As such, I feel you would be best suited for another position…."

Yes, ouch. But think about it this way. As difficult as it is, you are providing a needed service for that person: the opportunity for some realistic perspective that might prompt a career change in his best interest. Down the road, when he is installed in a job that fits him like a glove, one where he excels, he might thank you for doing the hard thing but the right thing.

### #6: Pursue excellence, never perfection.

Great leaders set high standards and pursue excellence in doing their work. But they don't try to attain perfection. What's the difference?

### Thoughts of a Successful Leader

The secret of joy in work
is contained in one word—excellence.
To know how to do something well is to enjoy it.

PEARL S. BUCK, AMERICAN WRITER

*Excellence* is a process where you work to achieve your very best in one or multiple arenas. When you are a person of excellence, you always seek to improve your skills and better yourself as a person. You view that search as part of an invigorating life journey.

*Perfection,* per *Merriam-Webster's,* is "the quality or state of being perfect…a degree of accuracy…that cannot be bettered."[9]

When you achieve perfection, you've arrived. There's no more work to do. But there's a problem with that. There's no such thing as perfect on this earth. Trying to achieve such a state is an exercise in frustration and futility. Those who strive to attain perfection will always be defeated.

A great leader realizes that sometimes things will go well on the path to pursuing excellence. Other times they won't. When things go well, he gives credit where credit is due—to his team. They celebrate their success together. When things don't go well, he accepts the responsibility. He gives his team straightforward information about what worked and what didn't work. Then he puts failure in perspective. "I guess we've found one way that doesn't work. So now let's find a way that does. I welcome your ideas, so put your thinking caps on."

When colleagues aren't pursuing excellence, he pulls them aside privately in a respectful conversation. It runs the way he'd want someone to approach him if he made a mistake or was short-sighted. He calmly addresses the facts and the behavior. He knows that behavior doesn't happen in a vacuum. There is always a why behind it. Once he peels back the layers to get to that why, he can engage the person with what I call a "teachable moment."

It's simple. All a leader has to do is step back and let natural consequences kick in. Reality will do the teaching. Sure, those consequences might sting a little, but the best way to learn anything is firsthand. It's up to the person to realize that if she decides to carry out her responsibilities with excellence, she'll be better off.

When the leader sees her doing better, he comments on it to encourage her onward and upward. "I noticed that you are working hard to adhere to your deadlines on this project. That must feel good." Or "Your presentation this morning was creative and informational. I can tell you spent a lot of time ensuring you could communicate the heart of your idea."

In doing so, that leader role-models through his words and actions that one mistake or one failure does not mean *you* are a mistake or a failure. Life can and does go on.

None of us can be perfect. But we can all choose to pursue excellence.

### Reinventing Success

My friend Herb Kelleher, the former chairman of the board of Southwest Airlines, was a great example of an authoritative leader. Repeatedly voted as the best CEO in the airline industry, Kelleher was an entrepreneurial force who stated that he knew nothing about airlines in the beginning. However,

> One mistake or one failure does not mean *you* are a mistake or a failure. Life can and does go on.

he ended up revolutionizing the airline industry to make travel affordable to the average customer. *CNN Business* called him "brilliant, charming, cunning, and tough."[10]

What those who worked with him remember most, though, is his legacy of connection. As one Southwest CEO said about Kelleher, "He inspired people; he motivated people; he challenged people—and, he kept us laughing all the way."[11] Kelleher's mantra? "If you take care of your people, they will take care of your customers, which will take care of your shareholders."[12]

*Forbes* called Kelleher a "pioneer, fierce competitor, and innovator."[13] But, most of all, "He changed the world…with a disruptive business model and a hard-to-replicate culture."[14] Kelleher showed the world that "it is possible to love people (employees and customers alike), have fun and make money simultaneously," believing he'd "rather have a company bound by love than a company bound by fear."[15]

When asked how he made Southwest a success, Kelleher answered, "Well, the people did it. I just stayed out of the way."[16]

He said that it was important to be there when they had problems but that his policy was to stay out of the way when things were going well. "Power should be reserved for weightlifting and boats," he quipped.[17]

Sadly, my friend Herb Kelleher passed away in 2019. But his founding principles live on in the airline industry. In April 2024, when Southwest employees discovered that a bride-to-be and her attendants were on board for her bachelorette party, they made a surprise all-passenger announcement. They passed out napkins and asked any lady who had been married to write advice for the bride. Those employees had the entire plane cheering for the almost-bride.[18]

What is Kelleher's legacy? As *Forbes* reported:

> "For almost 30 years we've been asking, 'What if you could build a company that is as human as the human beings in it? What if you could create a culture that inspires passionate people to come to work fully awake, fully engaged, firing on all cylinders because they know they are doing epic work?'
> Herb did it."[19]

That sounds like a pretty good recipe for success to me. Doesn't it to you? And it could be broadened to work in any environment.

Whenever I think about the concept of success, I remember back to when I decided I no longer wanted to sell magazines. Instead I wanted whatever I did to help people and be *of value*. I still have that same drive today. If I can help people through what I do and be of value, at the end of my days I'll be able to rest easy. I will have fulfilled my life's purpose.

So let me ask you. What is your gauge for success? How do you want to be remembered? Write down your thoughts, and let's get there together.

## Winning Play #3
## Know Those You Serve,
## and Serve Those You Know

*Kick-start motivation, creative problem-solving,
and a beneficial-for-all community.*

Recently I had the joy of passing out bumper stickers to parents in the parking lot of one of the Leman Academy of Excellence schools. I smiled and asked them one question as I handed over that sticker: "Are we taking good care of your family?" It was 105 degrees that day in Tucson, Arizona. I was in that parking lot for hours without a hat. (Don't tell my dermatologist.)

You might wonder why on earth I did that. Couldn't I have had someone else hand out those stickers? Yes, I could have. But I didn't want to. You see, I believe that a leader needs to be visible. If you aren't visible, how can you get to know people? And if you don't interact, how can you understand how they view the world?

I have seen many CEOs who think and act like head honchos. But they couldn't be more wrong. A CEO should be the biggest servant that company has. You have to serve those you know (your colleagues), and you have to know those you serve (your clients).

Decades of being a psychologist and counselor have convinced me that unless you approach people by recognizing *their* needs, *their* wants, and *their* values, you won't even get up to bat, much less to first base. You have to deal with others in a way that's consistent with how they view life.

That's why I believe relationships are at the heart of leadership. If you want your colleagues to achieve their personal bests, you need to first glimpse the world through their eyes as a unique individual. In Monday's chapter we explored the basics of birth order. When you understand birth order, you're way ahead of the game of the majority of leaders. Now you know why your colleagues and customers act like they do. That knowledge will come in mighty handy at work and anywhere else you encounter people.

In this chapter we're going to take things further. How does a person's birth order impact their work style? And what do individuals of each birth order need most from you? We'll discuss the ABCs every person craves and the 7 Essential Vitamins you should dole out liberally. Equipped with this knowledge, you'll become a five-star leader in any arena.

### *Thoughts of a Successful Leader*

Knowing your customer means
knowing what your customer really wants.
Maybe it is your product,
but maybe there's something else too:
Recognition, respect, reliability, concern, service,
a feeling of self-importance, friendship, help.

HARVEY MACKAY, AMERICAN CEO AND AUTHOR,
SWIM WITH THE SHARKS WITHOUT BEING EATEN ALIVE

### How Birth Order Impacts Work Style and Relationships

You're setting up a new committee. The stakes are high. It is imperative the people you choose can land the project. From experience, you know some colleagues are not easy to get along with. You also need fresh ideas to knock that project out of the ballpark. Which people should you ask to work together? It's helpful to know how the birth orders interact.

Group two firstborns and you'll have more than initial frustration. They'll spend most of their time arguing about their ideas. You might hear a volcanic eruption or two. With both determined to prove who's right and who's wrong, they'll have difficulty landing a decision. If they do, they'll struggle to get that project off the ground since they'll be nitpicking the details.

Assign two lastborns, and you'll hear lots of laughter. They'll shoot the breeze all afternoon instead of tackling that assignment. When you ask how the project brainstorming is coming, their response will be, "Project? What project?" Even when they do brainstorm, they'll likely have difficulty landing one idea that's workable or coming up with next steps.

Choose two middleborns, and they'll be comfortable because they understand how the other operates. However, since they're schooled by life to be peacemakers, neither will want to provide questions or potential negative feedback in response to the other's ideas. Getting a single workable idea may be difficult.

Put a middleborn next to a firstborn or a lastborn, though, and you'll get a winning combination. Since middleborns are highly adjustable mediators, they can most easily navigate the perfectionistic firstborn and the happy-go-lucky lastborn. When brainstorming concepts, a firstborn can get overly fixated on details. A middleborn can move discussion along without offending that firstborn. Middleborns can also kindly reign in a lastborn's party personality by subtle reminders to stay on track.

See how helpful knowing a bit about birth order can be? It puts you in the driver's seat in organizing projects and people and keeps you off the hot seat a greater majority of the time. When you carefully consider who you might group together, how they will respond to the work, and the ways they are likely to interact, you won't have to mediate as many personnel clashes.

## What Each Birth Order Needs Most from You

Sometimes sidewalks are straight. Sometimes they zigzag. Artistic walks can be round circles, look like snakes in the grass, or be dotted with handprints or footprints. What do they have in common? They all have borders.

> Which people should you ask to work together? It's helpful to know how the birth orders interact.

It is your job as leader to keep in mind the uniqueness of each of your colleagues while supplying those borders. Borders include your high standards, high expectations, and high level of support. They also include the type of culture you intentionally establish and how you choose to relate to others.

What happens within those borders as colleagues learn, explore, and discover how to achieve their personal bests will vary greatly based on individual gifts, skills, and experience in their fields. Some colleagues will follow the path you expect. Others will surprise you.

Take Mama Leman, whose final grade in algebra was the same as mine: 22 out of 100. Yet she ended up becoming a beloved nurse and, later, the hardworking superintendent of a convalescent home for children. No wonder she had the patience and foresight to believe the best of her son despite all evidence to the contrary. She had seen miracles in her own life.

Why is it so important to understand what each birth order needs most from you? If colleagues feel a personal connection and believe you are invested in their views, experiences, well-being, and growth, they are much more likely to do their work well. They will listen to your directions, live up to your standards and expectations, and assist in a smoothly running environment. In short, being proactive puts out behavioral fires before they flare up.

We'll take a look at each birth order's needs next.

### Firstborns and Onlies

A quick recap: Firstborns and onlies are detailed perfectionists who bear the standard for their families. They are often in the spotlight whether they want to be or not. They are highly critical of themselves, fear failure, and are reticent to take risks.

What do firstborns and onlies need most?

- Unconditional love, acceptance, and respect.

- To know their place in the group is secure and that they are regarded as a valued, contributing member.

- The opportunity to share thoughts, feelings, opinions, and research, but not to always be in the spotlight.

- To know they don't need to be perfect. The world won't end if they make a mistake or miss a deadline despite their best efforts.

- To be told that failure is okay. It's a natural part of learning and figuring out what *does not* work, so they can figure out next what *can* work.

- To know that they don't have to pick up after others who drop the ball. People are responsible and accountable for their own choices.

- To know that they don't have to do everything they are asked to do. They can present their case for which projects best match their skills.

- For others to realize that criticism is not only deeply hurtful, but it can also be deadly and paralyzing.

Firstborns and onlies are already hard enough on themselves.

- To be allowed some space and quiet to regroup and think more deeply before having to voice their opinions or thoughts.

- Time to talk one-on-one with you and other people more experienced in the field.

Remember that details and gathering information have always been important in the firstborn and only worlds. Provide opportunities for that, and they will thrive. They also spent the first years or more of their lives flying solo with those parental eyes on them. Showing interest in *their* thoughts and ideas, without forcing them to share, will make them more comfortable and encourage risk-taking of their well-thought-through brainstorms.

### Middleborns

A quick recap: Middle children are those squeezed between the Star firstborn and Little Ms. Drama Queen baby. They are often cast unwillingly in the role of "Family Mediator" between siblings. They are the least likely to be asked, "What do you think?" and are very loyal to their community group.

What do middleborns need most?

- Unconditional love, acceptance, and respect.

- To know their place in the group is secure and that they are regarded as a valued, contributing member.

- To know that what they think and feel matters and to be asked their thoughts, feelings, and opinions since they are not likely to volunteer them.

- To be allowed opportunities to develop a core group of social contacts and work partners.

- To know that it's not only okay to voice opinions and thoughts, but it's also valuable for others to hear their perspective.

- To know that it's not only right but good for them to speak up and stand up for themselves.

- To be encouraged to pursue their specific areas of strength.

- To know they don't have to play peacemaker between colleagues. Those big boys and girls should work it out themselves.

- Time to spend one-on-one with you as a leader showing interest in them as individuals.

Remember that middleborns had to work hard to carve a place in their growing-up homes. They were forced, sometimes out of self-preservation, to settle skirmishes when they only wanted household peace. That's why a face-to-face sit-down will be uncomfortable. Such a set-up will feel like a confrontation, which middleborns avoid at all costs. Their mental walls will already be ironclad against any invasion of you getting to know them.

What's a good strategy? Try talking as you walk down the office corridor or outside the building. Or take a coffee break and enjoy that brew sitting side-by-side on a park bench. If you do, and you sit quietly for a moment, enjoying your colleague's company, you'll be amazed what you learn when her mouth opens of her own free will.

### Lastborns

A quick recap: Lastborns are the babies of the family who thrive in the spotlight. Because of their charming, fun-loving personalities, they make friends easily. They have a lot of good ideas but sometimes lack follow-through. They are used to not being taken seriously but want others to take them seriously.

What do lastborns need most?

- Unconditional love, acceptance, and respect.

- To know their place in the group is secure and that they are regarded as a valued, contributing member.

- To know their unique contributions are not only wanted but needed in the group.

- To learn that life isn't a party 24/7. Sometimes they have to do real work too.

- To learn how to think through consequences before they act.

- To realize they don't have to be the center of attention. Others deserve a spotlight too.

- To learn that deadlines don't get done on their own but must be tackled with gusto.

- To learn that if they don't follow given rules or parameters, accountability follows.

- To learn that charm can only take you so far. Tactics that might have worked at home won't win friends among their colleagues.

- To be treated with respect so they will rise to the challenge.

- To be allowed to use their natural entertaining skills to help others laugh and de-stress.

- To have work be fun, with opportunities for social interaction through partnerships.

Remember that a lively environment is extremely important to lastborns. When they have it, they will perform like happy-go-lucky seals and charm even the most difficult of colleagues or customers. Without the fun factor though, work motivation will deflate like a pin-pricked balloon. So why not introduce and allow a little fun? You'll engage and perk up your entire community, especially those lastborns.

When you address the needs of each of the birth orders and develop your relational connection based on them, you'll build trust and respect. That partnership will spread exponentially to those you serve and who serve with you. That's because you as leader have the greatest power to shape that environment.

Your attitude and actions set the temperature of the room. The higher the relational connection with you, the more your colleagues know that, no matter what surprises come their way, you will be their staunch advocate. You won't waffle or back down in your support. Nor will you compromise on the culture you've intentionally designed. Your borders are firm, your values don't change, and the goals you set are high but attainable.

---

### LEMANISM #9
Engage with others in such a way
that every person thinks he or she is your favorite.

---

Now I want you to do something for me. Look at the first two bulleted items under each "What do (birth order) need most?" question. Don't they look familiar? Even repetitive?

You're right. They're the same under each category. I'll explain why next.

### What Everybody Needs and Wants Most

Every person on planet Earth has three core needs. I call them the ABCs. But they're not the alphabet you began reciting when

> Remember
> the ABCs
> *Acceptance
> *Belonging
> *Competence

you were knee high to a grasshopper. They are these. Every person wants to be Accepted, to Belong somewhere, and to be viewed as Competent in their ability to contribute. If you craft your environment to meet the ABCs, you'll never go wrong.

*Acceptance*

Contrary to how it might seem sometimes, your colleagues crave your approval. They want you to accept them as individuals with their diverse personalities and talents. They *want* to live up to your expectations. That little secret is why it's paramount to set high expectations and give colleagues the opportunity to rise rather than fall to your expectations. When you do so, you show them respect.

Doing things for others that they should do for themselves doesn't do them or you any favors. However well-intentioned you might be, such actions tell them, "I view you as dumb and inept. I don't think you can do it by yourself, so I have to help you." Such an approach won't grow their motivation or problem-solving skills or build their trust in you or respect for you.

> Your
> colleagues
> crave your
> approval.

Instead, be their champion. Adopt a "Go for it! I know you can do it because I believe in you" attitude. Use verbal and written encouragement lavishly. Your colleagues' kites will fly higher on that wind than you can imagine and keep going for a long time. People want to be noticed, listened to, liked, and feel special. A smile, a nod, a friendly glance, a kind word, or a note is all it takes to influence a life forever. Isn't that worth a few minutes of your time?

## Work It Out

### Dealing with Difficult People

Let's be honest. Some people are easier to like than others. Here's the rub. Your colleagues instinctively know if you don't like them. So do their peers.

A negative interaction tends to be only seconds long.[20] It might be words like, "That isn't important right now. Catch me later" or "I expected more from you." It might include calling out a person in front of his peers.

But did you know it takes *five* positive interactions to offset the impact of *one* negative interaction?[21] That's why it's wise to think before you speak or act. If you need to hold a colleague accountable, never do it publicly. Pull aside that person *privately*. Talk *with* rather than *at* her. Never accuse, nag, or belittle her.

Instead, calmly address the detrimental behavior in a relational style. Say, "I could be wrong, but I think you might have done X (a specific action) because of X (root cause of the behavior)," or "I've noticed you seem unhappy working on that team. I'd like to hear your thoughts if you're willing to share them."

Think of your most difficult colleague or client. How did your last interaction go? Why do you think it played out that way? How might you respond differently now?

## Belonging

Every person longs to belong somewhere. We all desire a community we can identify with and who will support us. What's critical is *where* we choose to belong.

> Every person longs to belong somewhere.

Your colleagues need to know they play unique roles within your community. One may be a stellar researcher who brings new perspective. Another might be the master of traversing wildly differing ideas to come up with a terrain all can agree on and walk together. Still another's friendly, memorable way of treating customers causes them to return to your location in droves.

Be intentional about ensuring and nurturing each colleague's unique role. Self-worth grows when individuals work hard to do what they do best and are able to see the beneficial results within the group they belong to. People will never feel secure as part of your community unless they are able to contribute, are recognized, and are appreciated for their combination of skills. A little appreciation can go a very long way.

## Competence

Want your colleagues to gain psychological muscle to power over any hurdle? Empower them by giving them responsibility and holding them accountable. When you do, you send a message: "I believe you are competent to do this task and to do it well."

As we all know, some people will race through that job to the finish line. Others will inch at a snail's pace. Still others will lollygag through the daisies. Some might not finish at all, despite your roadmap and high expectations.

For colleagues who get to the finish line, you say, "Good job. I bet it feels great to complete that project." If you see ways to make improvements, give feedback positively in a private setting, especially with firstborns and onlies. They are their own worst enemies as critics. They already know what they'd do differently next time after running through the project steps a bazillion times in their head. They don't need you to point out their flaws. Other colleagues, though, may need a kind suggestion or two.

For those who don't complete the task or do it poorly, allow reality to do the teaching. When the customer shows up, that colleague has to be the one who says, "I apologize, sir. Your car isn't ready yet. I dropped the ball in not calling you and giving you an update." You as a leader don't rescue him from being the news bearer.

You also don't rescue him from the hot seat as he strategizes how to appease that not-so-happy customer. Instead you wait. You listen and affirm his solution when he says, "I agreed to give him $100 off his order and to drop off the car myself at his home tomorrow."

> Want your colleagues to gain psychological muscle to power over any hurdle? Empower them by giving them responsibility and holding them accountable.

When you treat that colleague as competent, you don't let him off the hook. He receives $100 less for his commission, and he has to deliver that car at the end of the day tomorrow on his own time. That is part and parcel of him learning to take his responsibility seriously and you holding him accountable.

Either way, your colleagues learn something.

Those who complete the task well learn how good it feels to work hard and call a project their own. On top of that, the leader whose approval they seek gives them a figurative pat on the back with a "Good job." With such encouragement it's no wonder their ears remain wide open for suggested improvements on the next project.

In the second scenario, a colleague learns firsthand what happens when he drops an important ball and doesn't give a sale his best shot. He experiences the uncomfortable, inconvenient, real-life consequences. It doesn't take a brain scientist to realize that did not go well. Nine times out of 10 he'll decide to do things differently next time.

Some of you are saying right now, "But Dr. Leman, you don't understand my industry. I could never let an employee make a mistake." I hear you. Some work has higher stakes than others. But consider this: Would you rather such a situation happened only once? Next time the stakes might be even higher. If you want to keep that colleague onboard, now is the time to learn. If his skills clearly aren't a match for your venture, that's a different conversation.

Using the ABCs supports and empowers your colleagues. When colleagues feel they are accepted, belong to your community, and that you see them as competent, self-worth grows. Relationships flourish. Problem-solving comes more naturally. Failures are learning experiences. Colleagues become more confident in tackling responsibilities and mastering challenges.

Why not try out the ABCs this week? Focus on **A**cceptance, **B**elonging, and **C**ompetence, and soon they will become second nature. Use those ABCs along with the 7 Essential Vitamins we'll talk about next, and you'll have a "we win together" atmosphere where you and all your colleagues can thrive.

### *Thoughts of a Successful Leader*

Motivation is the art of getting people to do what you want them to do because they want to do it.

DWIGHT D. EISENHOWER, 34TH PRESIDENT OF THE UNITED STATES, SUPREME COMMANDER ALLIED EXPEDITIONARY FORCE IN EUROPE, WORLD WAR II

## The 7 Essential Vitamins

Want your colleagues to grow to their full potential? Then use these 7 Essential Vitamins in generous doses. Distribute them widely, and you'll be amazed at the transformation.

### *Vitamin A = Accountability + Attitude*

If you want people to become responsible, give them responsibility and hold them accountable for completing their tasks with a good attitude. Doing too much for your colleagues and rescuing them from consequences will backfire. It will create chaos in your community and with your customers.

It will also hamper that colleague's long-term success in other areas. What company or committee down the road wants a person who has a bad attitude? Who can't play well with others? Who passes the buck of blame when he's caught not finishing his projects? Who can't contribute positively to the community?

---

**LEMANISM #10**
Don't fall for excuses.
Excuses make the weak weaker.

---

A hovered-over late-blooming plant will never bloom with too much watering. It will merely become limp and unable to stand up under harsh conditions in the real world. So do your colleagues a favor. Give them responsibility. Hold them accountable. Set clear guidelines, high standards, and high expectations. Treat them as competent.

Then back off and let those colleagues make their own decisions. Will they be responsible? You can't *make* people have a good attitude. Neither can you *make* them be responsible. But you can hold them accountable for their actions.

Colleagues must choose whether to learn the hard way or the easy way. The sooner they learn that attitude matters and has consequences, the better. One choice is 100% certain. Finishing a project on deadline and doing your best will always lead to a sense of accomplishment and grow self-worth.

### Thoughts of a Successful Leader

You cannot tailor-make the situations in life, but you can tailor-make the attitudes to fit those situations.

Zig Ziglar, American Motivational Speaker and Author

### Vitamin B = Behavioral Expectation

If you expect the worst, you'll likely get that. But if you expect the best, you're much more likely to get that. So why not expect the best so you have the highest probability to get the best?

A colleague has difficulty finishing her tasks. You know a big deadline is coming up in two days. You pull her aside in the empty break room and offer her a mug of her favorite tea. "I really look forward to seeing your complete draft on Wednesday. I know it's a lot of work. But I chose you specifically for that project because I believe you have the unique skills to pull it off. If you want to run anything by me before then, let me know. If not, that's okay too. I'll look forward to viewing the finished draft in two days with our clients."

After such words, chances are pretty high that colleague will show up prepared for that presentation. She'll be in intense work mode for the next two days and might even pull some evening hours or an all-nighter to land the project. Why? Because you have established a relational connection. Remember, she wants your approval. She wants you to be happy with her. She'll go that extra mile because you spurred her on with relational motivation.

Contrast that with this approach. You stride down the hallway and pause at her desk. "Miranda, your project is due in two days. *Two days.* From what I see, I don't think you're close to being done, but you'd better be. The clients will be here Wednesday afternoon at 3:00 p.m. I want to be completely clear here. Your job is on the line. Miss the mark, and you're out." You swivel and power back toward your office.

What have you done? You've planted the seed in Miranda's mind to *not* finish that project. She was already feeling discouraged because she dawdled and couldn't make up her mind how to tackle the project. Now she might as well give up. She'll never be able to pull it off perfectly with the deadline. You've stripped her of all motivation.

On Wednesday, who's embarrassed in front of the clients? It's you. Miranda is a no-show. To add complexity, you're also forced to comply with your threat of firing her. Problem is, she's working steadily on another project with a tight deadline and is the only one on your team with the skills to do it. You've created a sticky mess of cobwebs. If you don't say what you mean and do what you say, why would she or any other colleague trust you?

Instead, go for great expectations. They don't guarantee you'll *always* get the best, but they can make a great difference. Try them out and see.

---

**LEMANISM #11**

People live up to the expectations
you have for them.

---

### Vitamin C = Caring + Cooperation

A tough but good-hearted football coach once told me about his players, "They don't care what you know…until they know that you care." The same goes for those you serve and who serve with you. They don't care what you know, or what you think, or what you say until they know you care.

The words you choose to use directly impact how your colleagues listen to and engage with you. They also influence how willing they are to do the work and to contribute positively to the group. Caring starts with getting behind their eyes to understand how they view the world and their role in it. It solidifies when you choose to uniquely connect with each person.

> The words you choose to use directly impact how your colleagues listen to and engage with you.

When you care, you are available for and welcome one-on-one conversations. You empathize with their life struggles and are sensitive to what matters to them. Yes, that's a tall order when you have more than a few colleagues and customers. But there's no replacement for a caring leader when it comes to winning others' cooperation.

### Vitamin D = Discipline

As a leader, do you model a disciplined life? Do you stay in control even when you're upset? Do you focus on actions you're unhappy with rather than the actors? Do you finish tasks you dread without procrastinating? Do you do what you say you will do when you say you will do it?

The instant you step into leadership, you become a role model. People are watching you. What you do will shout more loudly than what you say. What do you do when things don't go as expected? What method will you use to get that colleague back on track?

*Punishment* swiftly handles the immediate situation with a dash of retribution and revenge. Threats of far worse consequences are thrown in for good measure. The spotlight is on the person rather than the detrimental act. For example, "I expected better of you as a professional."

> What you do will shout more loudly than what you say.

*Discipline* allows real-life consequences for actions. A leader who is in healthy authority addresses the situation from a long-term perspective. She focuses on the action rather than the person. What happened? Why did it happen? What steps could you take for this not to happen again? Discipline has bettering the colleague and his work in mind.

If you don't have a relationship before things don't go as expected, it's much more difficult to problem-solve and get back on track. That's why I believe highly in what I call "relational discipline." We'll explore that more on Thursday.

### Vitamin E= Encouragement

There's a mountain of difference between *praise* and *encouragement*. Even dictionaries know. Let's take a look.

*Praise*

1. To express a favorable **judgment** of;
2. To glorify especially by the attribution of **perfections.**
3. An expression of **approval.**[22]

*Encouragement*

1. The action of giving someone **support, confidence,** or **hope.**
2. The act of trying to **stimulate** the development of an activity, state, or belief.[23]
3. To **inspire with courage.**[24]

Note the words highlighted in bold for *praise*: *judgment, perfections,* and *approval.* Praise sounds like it would be positive, but it's actually negative. It focuses on the doer and how that person measures up. It sets expectations so high that the person is on shaky ground and primed for a fall.

Now note the words highlighted in bold for *encouragement: support, confidence, hope, stimulate, inspire with courage.* Encouragement is positive through and through. It focuses on the deed or action and on how the person feels about that action.

Here's an example:

*Praise:* "You nailed that project. Nobody in the world could have pulled that off as fast or as well as you did. You're the best engineer in the whole world!"

*Encouragement:* "All that studying, research, and night class really helped with this project. Your hard work and extra effort is greatly appreciated. I bet you feel a huge sense of accomplishment. Congratulations on nailing the project with excellence."

People instinctively sense the difference between praise and encouragement. They can't be fooled. Praise puts a colleague in the precarious position of having to maintain a perfect position every day. Firstborns and onlies, in particular, will feel a lot of stress. They may become very driven to succeed or procrastinate out of fear of being criticized for failing to reach the high bar. They may become discouraged since they know that someone could come along tomorrow and knock them right off their pedestal.

> Praise = NO
> Encouragement = YES

A colleague who feels the internal success of knowing she did something well as a result of her hard work will always outshine a colleague who is praised. That's because the sweetest words to anyone's heart are these encouraging ones: "I care about you. I believe in you. I have confidence in you. I know you can do this."

### Vitamin L = Laughter

Laughter is an essential ingredient to a well-rounded environment. Having fun together gels a group, provides acceptance and belonging, and lessens the probability of disputes. Those who have fun together are more likely to have each other's backs and help each other out. They feel more comfortable in sharing ideas, research, and contacts.

A chuckle or two can take the edge off intense situations so all can refocus on the subject at hand, minus detrimental emotion. When word gets around that your hard-working, successful department is also the "fun one," other leaders might risk lightening up a little too.

A smile is contagious. Laughter is even more so. In fact, it's the best infection to catch.

### Vitamin N= No

*No* isn't a dirty word. In fact, it's not only useful but necessary. Not every idea is a good idea. Not every behavior is beneficial, nor is it healthy. Saying no when you need to assists in drawing clear boundaries so colleagues know what to expect. If they step over a certain boundary, then the simple A+B=C equation applies. You don't need to nag, raise your voice, smooth things over, or remind.

Will colleagues be happy when you use vitamin N? No, of course not. But no one should get their way all the time. Always saying yes is a disservice because it's an illusion that won't hold up in real life.

When should you say yes, and when should you say no? Say yes when you can and when the situation allows for it. Save your no for what really matters. When colleagues know your no means no, and that you won't change your mind, you lessen the potential for confusion or arguments.

For those of you who struggle to say no because you worry about hurting someone's feelings, I have an exercise for you. Stand in front of a mirror. Form the letters N-O. Then say them out loud until you can do so without flinching.

Today's the day to discover the freeing power of no.

## Work It Out

### It's All about Role-Modeling

1. If you want accountability and attitude, model accountability and attitude.

2. If you set the bar high in behavioral expectation, model that standard.

3. If caring and cooperation is important to you, live those values.

4. If you want a hard-working, disciplined group, be hard-working and disciplined.

5. If you want a culture of encouragement, be an encourager.

6. If you want people to stay for the long haul, don't forget the fun factor.

7. If you want people to trust you, use your yes and your no wisely.

### Service with a Smile

Not too long ago I talked with a veteran insurance agent about the secret to his success. When he gets a new client, he asks about the family. He notes birthdays, anniversaries, special details, and upcoming events. When he contacts that client, he says, "How is Jaden doing in her new job?" or, "How did Jack's high school graduation go?" And he always asks, "Is there anything I can do for you?"

That insurance agent understands that leadership is personal. It's personal to you, and it's personal to all you come in contact with. A great leader is service-oriented and has a servant's heart. He knows his most important mantra is "Relationship first, relationship always." How you serve someone has everything to do with how she feels about you, her work, and how she interacts with others.

A great leader knows he must choose his words carefully if he wants colleagues and customers to listen and engage with him. Talking in a friendly manner on the fly is one thing. But there's nothing like the power of the handwritten note.

---

## LEMANISM #12
The words you choose to use matter greatly.

---

These days, no one gets many handwritten notes. On the rare occasions you do, you're likely impressed because such notes show extra effort. They're not emails or texts you can dash off in a few seconds. If you mail them, you have to find or buy a stamp. There's something about seeing writing on paper that gives it a weighty feel of permanence. For all these reasons, the effects of handwritten notes can be profound and lasting.

Yes, time is a precious commodity. Most of us don't have enough of it. But why not write that encouraging note today? Share meaningful specifics. Remember birthdays, anniversaries, and other events. Such efforts will build foundations, open doors, and break down walls. The next time you have a hard push on a project and need extra help, which colleague do you think will spend a few extra hours to help you out?

A great leader knows that people don't care what you know until they know that you care. When you care enough to understand and uniquely connect with people, you build relationships that will triumph over annoyances and mistakes and stand strong in all kinds of weather. As a bonus, when you lift others up, you are more joyful too. Never underestimate the power of a smile, a simple hello, or positive words.

If you were asked to give a 10-second recipe for leadership success, what would you say? Here is mine: "Choose your words wisely. Use the power of the handwritten note. Show that you care about that unique individual. And always, always put relationships first."

## Thoughts of a Successful Leader

If you could only sense how important you are
to the lives of those you meet; how important you can
be to the people you may never even dream of.
There is something of yourself that you leave
at every meeting with another person.

FRED ROGERS, AMERICAN TELEVISION HOST

## Winning Play #4
## Refine Your Leadership Strategies

*Discover purposive behavior, relational discipline,*
*and how to win cooperation.*

What would you do with these three colleagues, if you were their leader?

Molly has always been steady and trustworthy. She's been with your company for seven years in middle management, and she's good at it. Her rapport with others is stellar. When division brews, she is able to move the parties to a mutually satisfying solution. She is organized and prepared, calm in crisis, and fair in her decision-making. Her team members feel respected and heard because she is relational and caring.

But over the past week, she has acted withdrawn. The last two days she's been 20 minutes late to work. Your nationwide company has a policy of writing warnings for late arrivals starting with the third occurrence. Five warnings could mean dismissal. You hate to write her up. Should you say something now? Or hope this is only a fluke and wait it out?

Then there's Jonas, who has been with you for a year. He's a quiet, exceptional worker who plays by the rules. Problem is, you've noticed he still doesn't mingle with colleagues except when he has to. He remains at his desk during break times and eats a yogurt while continuing to work. You believe community is important. How can you prompt him to engage?

Finally, there's Rebecca, a bright star for the last three years. No colleague has learned the ropes faster. Lately, though, she's edging toward troublemaker status. She still finishes her work well but seems antsy, even bored. In meetings, she sometimes boldly questions your leadership. Her most recent question was, "Are you sure that's the right approach for that project?"

Leaders face quandaries like these every day, and they have to choose what they will do next. We already briefly explored the three types of leadership styles on Tuesday. In this chapter, we'll look at how your style choice directly influences the strategies you choose to use. We'll explore the reasons for behavior and how you can turn detrimental behaviors around with discipline the Leman Way. It's easy to use and works every time... guaranteed.

## How Leadership Style Influences Strategy

If you choose an authoritarian or permissive style, you will tend to *react* to situations. Reacting is that instinctive gut action you take based on the input you currently have. You engage in words or actions before the thought of consequences kicks in. You simply do what comes naturally. And let's be honest. Sometimes it feels really good in the moment, doesn't it? But the fallout later...well, that's not such a good feeling.

> You can turn detrimental behaviors around with discipline the Leman Way. It's easy to use and works every time... guaranteed.

Take a look at how each of the three styles would respond in the situations with Molly, Jonas, and Rebecca.

Authoritarians would write an unofficial warning and slap it on Molly's desk to get her attention and force her back on track. They would go to Jonas's desk during break time and insist he go to the break room. They would tell Rebecca, "Of course I'm sure. I'm the leader, and you will handle that project my way. You need to get on board with the plan."

Using do-it-my-way-or-else control with an undertone of warning or threat is never a good idea. Such an approach breeds resentment and rebellion, not to mention the specter of civil lawsuits. In fact, if Rebecca had an authoritarian leader, I wouldn't be surprised if she attempted a *coup d'état* in the next week or two.

Permissive leaders would say to Molly, "You don't seem to be yourself. Am I giving you too much work? Can I help? I could do a portion of your project. You seem so tired. Why don't you rest a bit in the morning and come in when you feel like it next week?" Such an approach intends to solve what is bothering Molly and impeding her work. However, it too is a form of control and an invasion of privacy that breeds resentment and rebellion. Molly is not given the opportunity to give input. Instead, the leader assesses the facts and pronounces the solution(s).

> If you choose an authoritarian or permissive style, you will tend to *react* to situations.

For her part, Molly is thinking, *I wish she would leave me alone. Things are stressful enough. I need time to figure out how to solve this. She makes it worse by throwing solutions I feel like I have to respond to right now.* As a typically well-organized person, Molly also feels guilty for not adhering to her usual standards. She's embarrassed that someone noticed. She thought she was doing a good job hiding her discouragement.

A permissive leader would hover over Jonas's desk like a well-intentioned vulture at break time. "I know you don't usually go to break, but you're really missing out. C'mon, I won't take no for an answer. It's a lot of fun." So Jonas goes, but he certainly doesn't have fun. He has been *forced* to be social, and nobody on the planet likes that. What will he do next break time? Here's a likely option. He'll high-tail it to the restroom to sit in peace in one of those stalls.

What about Rebecca? A permissive leader would waffle and lose confidence. "Oh, well, I *thought* that would be the best way, but now I'm not so sure. What do you think, Rebecca?" Such a style opens the door for the breezy Rebecca to sweep in like a tsunami and knock down everything and everyone in her path to be acknowledged. Then, as the Brits say, "Bob's your uncle." It won't take long for others to look to her as the leader in those meetings.

---

**LEMANISM #13**

Never give up your authority
to *anyone* for *any* reason.

---

Authoritarian and permissive styles are both ways to exert control. Neither gives leaders time to think, *Is the information I have correct? Is there more I should know? What's the broader context? If I act now, what are the consequences to that person, my team, and myself?* That's why leaders with such styles often get open-mouth-insert-foot syndrome. Authoritarians won't apologize because they have to be right. Permissive leaders over-apologize and try to fix the situation because they want to be liked.

Authoritative leaders don't need to be in control. They are in control. They don't react, they *respond*. Before engaging in a fight, they take a mental or physical time-out. They don't speak on the fly or act in the heat of the moment. If you choose an authoritative style, you ask yourself, *how might I handle this situation for the greatest learning potential?* Sometimes the best way is to say, "Let me think about that, and I'll get back to you."

Authoritative leaders observe carefully and gather the facts. They listen but do not judge. They problem-solve by running scenarios as options and considering the consequences before they act. Most of all, they are always kind, straightforward, and relational.

An authoritative leader would privately approach Molly in a friendly, low-key fashion. "You do such great work, Molly. I want you to know how much I appreciate it. Like the time when (and he shares a specific example). You're able to accomplish so much by yourself. Just know that you don't always have to. I've got your back. If there's anything you want to share with me at any time, I'm all ears. I'd like to help if I can."

> If you choose an authoritative style, you ask yourself, *How might I handle this situation for the best learning potential?*

Note that he doesn't coerce an answer. He doesn't ask Molly a question that she feels compelled to answer. He merely thanks her for her work and leaves the door open for discussion should she choose to walk through it. It's up to Molly whether to talk now, later, or not at all. Such a respectful act leaves her in the driver's seat of what she decides to share.

In the case of Jonas, the authoritative leader would go to him during a break time when all colleagues are elsewhere. She would say, "Mind if I sit with you for a minute? I'm so glad you're on board with us. I greatly appreciate your work." She would detail ways in which he has specifically contributed his unique skills. "You know, the team we're on is amazing. For me, one of the greatest things about this company is finding a community to share the work I love with. I've learned so much from my colleagues. Like the time when…."

She would end with this encouragement: "When I first came to work here, I thought focusing on doing my job well was enough. I missed breaks to get work done. Now when I can't go to break, I miss it. There's nothing like laughing together to lighten the worst of days and put events in perspective. If you ever want someone to walk through that break room door with you, I'm game. Just give me a shout." Then she would smile and exit without fanfare, leaving the thoughtful Jonas with some new thoughts to ponder.

### Thoughts of a Successful Leader

Courage is what it takes to stand up and speak;
Courage is also what it takes to sit down and listen.

WINSTON CHURCHILL, BRITISH STATESMAN
AND FORMER PRIME MINISTER

What about Rebecca? Because other colleagues might have the same question but not be courageous enough to voice it, the authoritative leader would say, "That's a great question, Rebecca. Thanks for sharing it. There isn't always a right way or a wrong way to do our projects. They can be done in different ways. That's what makes them fun. They're never the same old thing, am I right?" He engages the group with laughter to draw them together.

Then he continues. "This project is not only new to us but complex. So, to answer your question, Rebecca, no, I'm not 100 percent sure this is the right approach. There are too many variables to make that claim, and I'd be dishonest in doing so. However, after talking with many of you about the best ways to proceed in areas of your fortes, I formed the plan you see in front of you. It's the plan we'll follow for now. If we need to make adjustments along the way, we'll do that as we always do." That leader then moves into explaining the roles each colleague will play as part of the taskforce.

---

**LEMANISM #14**
Authoritative leaders don't react.
They respond.

---

A great authoritative leader would also take a hint from that bold question. He'd let the dust from that meeting settle for a few hours and then privately approach Rebecca. He would thank her for the good question and ask if she had any other thoughts from the meeting. He would applaud her detailed thinking and say, "We have a new project coming up in a month. If you'd be willing to look at it and offer your thoughts in advance, I'd love to hear them."

A smart leader channels criticism into a positive force for change. Such an approach nips rebellious thinking in the bud and allows ideas to enter in an organized, monitored way that respects all your colleagues. Rebecca will have a new challenge for her abundant energy.

So let me ask you, which leadership style do you think would be the least stressful to you in the long run, and why? And if you were Molly, Jonas, or Rebecca, which style would you prefer your boss to have? Why?

## Why People Behave Like They Do

I've got a new word for your leadership vocabulary: *purposive.* I bet it isn't one you or anyone else in your circle has used today. But it's a very important word.

Want to change the behavior of your colleagues? Then you need to know that all behavior is *purposive.* It serves a purpose. People wouldn't do it unless they got something they want from that behavior. Here's the good news: remove that purpose, and there's no further need for that behavior.

### Thoughts of a Successful Leader

To be successful you must accept all challenges that come your way. You can't just accept the ones you like.

MICHAEL GAFKA, SENIOR WW BUSINESS STRATEGY MANAGER, HEWLETT PACKARD

When I was Assistant Dean of Students at the University of Arizona, Dori (not her real name) would come in my office and tattle on her colleague Mary about something or other. It became a pattern. In fact, I'd sigh every time I heard Dori's footsteps approaching.

It didn't take long for me to realize what was going on. After all, I am a psychologist. Every time Dori poked her head in to "share a concern I should know about," she was getting the stroke of attention she needed. Remember what I said about behavior being purposive?

It was time to remove that purpose. The next time she approached my doorway, I got proactive. I met her there. "Oh, hello, Dori. Come with me for a minute, would you?" I walked down the hallway with Dori next to me until we stood in front of Mary's desk.

"Good afternoon, Mary," I said, smiling. "Dori has something to tell you."

Dori's eyes widened. Her mouth worked, but nothing came out. Silence descended.

I left the two ladies for their own conversation. Never again did Dori share a concern about Mary with me. I noticed the two even ate lunch together sometimes. Problem solved.

As a bonus, word got around about how Dean Leman handled staff issues. Nobody wanted to be in Dori's shoes, so gossip stopped floating my way. My actions were simple. All I did was ask a person to walk a few feet down the hallway with me. Then I placed the ball of responsibility squarely in her court with six simple words: "Dori has something to tell you."

When you remove the payoff for the behavior, the behavior stops. That's why it's critical to get to the root cause of any behavior. Many leaders stop at the details of *what* happened *when*. Far more important is *why*. What does the actor gain from that behavior? When you know *why*, you'll be able to assist in resolving that detrimental behavior.

Sometimes all it takes is six words. Try them out and see the marvels they will accomplish.

---

**LEMANISM #15**

All behavior is *purposive.*
It serves a purpose.
Remove that purpose, and
there's no further need for that behavior.

---

## The Four Stages of Misbehavior[25]

Did you know all of us crave attention? We are created for connection. We want and need others to notice us. As kids, we sized up the social atmosphere and figured out how best to work the system.

Some of us did it by pleasing parents through achieving good grades, high ranks in sports, and lead chairs in orchestra. Others formed friend groups that gave us the attention and loyalty we desired. Yet others did it by helping people like the older neighbor who needed groceries and her lawn mowed. Still others of us drove the adults in our lives crazy with our antics. We forced them to pay attention for their own preservation. (That last one, by the way, was me, little Kevin Leman.)

This is *Stage 1: Attention.* At this stage a person believes, *I only count when I am being noticed or served.* If that person receives positive attention, she won't progress to the next stage. By positive attention, I don't mean unrealistic praise, such as, "Marilee, you are the best interior decorator ever." She knows that's not true.

Instead, I mean encouraging words like, "Marilee, I want to thank you for all your hard work in making our foyer so inviting to customers. You have a gift for making spaces look great. Seeing it makes everybody smile. I bet it makes you smile too."

Both statements are meant to give that colleague attention. However, the first one focuses on the person, setting her up in a precarious, competitive position. The second focuses on positive action she took that benefited the entire community.

> All of us crave attention.
> We are created for connection.
> We want and need others to notice us.

*Stage 2: Power.*[26] When people don't receive attention in a positive way, they will switch their tactics. They'll focus on getting attention in a negative way. They become power-driven, forcing you to pay attention to them. In this stage a person believes, *I only count when you do what I want or I can do what I want.*

Rebecca, who publicly challenged her boss about his method, is a clear example of a person in danger of moving to *Stage 2: Power.* She craves attention but is pursuing it in an unacceptable way. However, if an authoritative leader gives her attention for positive behaviors and a roadmap to increased responsibility, she's likely to remain in *Stage 1.*

*Stage 3: Revenge.* Those who move to *Stage 3* still want attention but have given up on positive attention. They are keenly focused on getting attention in a negative way. After all, any attempts to get attention for doing something good have completely failed.

Those in this stage believe, *I only count when I can hurt others as I have been hurt by life.* These are the colleagues who booby-trap their peers. They revenge-gossip on social media and don't consider the consequences. They purposefully blow their deadlines to hurt fellow team members. They sell company secrets without a qualm. They are also, tragically, the people you see headlined in the news as the perpetrators of mass shootings and other violence.

*Stage 4: Display of Inadequacy or Assumed Disability.* Those who move into this stage have given up and chosen to retreat from life. They are so discouraged that they don't show interest in anything. But instead of turning their lack of receiving attention outward, as those in *Stage 3* do, they turn it inward. They blame themselves. Persons in this stage believe, *I can't do anything right, so I won't try to do anything at all.* They add to that, *I'm no good.*

Through all these stages, behavior serves a purpose. But the root cause is a lack of positive attention. Do you see why I believe that giving attention in a positive way is one of the most important aspects of being a leader?

## The 4 Stages of Misbehavior

*Stage 1, Attention:* I only count when I am being noticed or served.

*Stage 2, Power:* I only count when you do what I want or I can do what I want.

*Stage 3, Revenge:* I only count when I can hurt others as I have been hurt by life.

*Stage 4, Display of Inadequacy or Assumed Disability:* I can't do anything right, so I won't try to do anything at all. I'm no good.

The good news is that 99 percent of colleagues who crave attention will remain in *Stage 1: Attention* or *Stage 2: Power.* How do I know? I've spent decades counseling many people in those stages. Those in *Stage 3* or *Stage 4* need more help than this book can give. They need professional assistance…and swiftly.

How can you tell the difference between an attention-seeker and a power-driven colleague? It's fairly easy.

Does the behavior *annoy* you? If so, he's an attention seeker.

Does the behavior *provoke* you? If so, he's power-driven.

Each of us makes mistakes. Each of us has flaws. Sometimes we need attitude and behavior adjustments. As I stated earlier, there's a big difference between *punishment* and *discipline.*

Punishment trains *down*. It focuses on revenge, the need to make someone pay. It's a short-term fix because it addresses only what, not why. Without pinpointing the root cause for the behavior, it will likely happen again. There's also an uncomfortable oops-factor. You're annoyed or infuriated by the instigator, so you *react*. You don't give yourself the opportunity to ensure you have all the facts or to ask yourself, *What would be the best way to handle this?*

Discipline handles mistakes and flaws in a positive manner that trains *up*. It prompts a person to stop misbehavior through understanding and experiencing real-life consequences. It gives her the opportunity to *choose* to make amends for any harm resulting from her actions or attitude and then to *choose* to respond differently if such a situation arises again. Discipline has the potential for long-term character growth with benefits far beyond the workplace.

> Punishment trains *down*.
> Discipline trains *up*.

But there's an even better way, the Leman Way. It works every single time in every situation. And there's a bonus: it will grow your relationship positively with that person too.

## The 7 Principles of Relational Discipline

You want your colleagues to have character, but sometimes you get colleagues who *are* characters. As a leader, I'm sure you know all about that. Relational discipline allows real-life consequences to do the teaching. You don't need to warn, threaten, or coerce. You simply let nature take its course. Then you quietly provide that teachable moment for a life lesson.

The goal of relational discipline is to create responsible, accountable people. But to do that, you first have to know and understand each colleague. If there's no relationship, he won't care what you think or what you do. The consequences of his actions and words won't matter as much, either. That's why Wednesday's Winning Play was, "Know those you serve, and serve those you know."

Relational discipline is based on actions, not words. It steers a course between the "my way or the highway" authoritarian and the permissive "what can I do for you?" styles. It is authoritative. It allows your colleagues to choose their responses and then holds them accountable for the consequences of those choices.

How does relational discipline work? Here is an example of how the Leman Way differs.

Your team is working on a month-long project. Once it's complete, you plan to surprise each member with a bonus for their hard work. One colleague drops the ball on the last day of the deadline. He takes a long lunch break and spends the majority of the day on his phone. By the end of the

> Relational discipline allows real-life consequences to do the teaching.

workday, he's not done with his portion. What do you do next?

An authoritarian leader would scold that colleague. "I told you it was due today, and it's not done. What's your problem? Was I not clear? You're going to stay tonight until it's done. No one is going to torch this project, not on my watch."

117

A permissive leader would say apologetically, "Oh, you're not done? Was your portion too much for you to do? Should I get others to help you? We're all in this together, you know."

An authoritative leader would say nothing. He'd let that not-so-working worker walk out the door blissfully unaware of the consequences. Then he'd approach Catherine, whom he can always count on. "You've worked so hard on this project, and we only have a little bit left. I'm asking for your assistance, but you can say no, and I won't be offended. Would you be willing to finish up the last part at home tonight? I estimate it'll take 2-3 hours. You're such a fast, efficient worker that you might get it done faster. Call me if you have any questions, and I'll be available."

You smile. "There's also a perk in it for you. Help me out tonight, and you can have the entire day off tomorrow, paid, to spend with your family, before you start your next project. How does that sound?"

Catherine does some quick math. *Spend 2-3 hours tonight while still having time with my family in exchange for having a full day off, paid. What a great deal. I could take the kids to the zoo since Tuesdays are free.* In the blink of an eye, she agrees. That night a highly motivated Catherine knocks out that project expertly in 1.5 hours after tucking the kids into bed. She goes to bed herself with sugarplums of a day off dancing in her head.

### Thoughts of a Successful Leader

The quality of our lives depends not on whether we have conflicts, but on how we respond to them.

THOMAS CRUM, MARTIAL ARTS AND CONFLICT RESOLUTION EXPERT

The next day you place handwritten notes and bonus checks on your colleagues' workstations. An excited buzz spreads. Smiles abound. But one colleague isn't smiling. In fact, he looks confused and upset. You observe that what's-up expression and head for your office. You want what happens next to occur privately out of respect for him.

He pauses at your office door and then knocks. "Boss? May I have a moment?"

"Sure," you say, and motion him in.

"Well, you know those bonuses? I think you forgot one. I didn't get an envelope."

Let the teachable moment begin. "No, I did not forget," you answer calmly. You turn your attention back to other papers on your desk.

"But my bonus is missing," he insists.

You look up and catch his gaze. "You did not receive a bonus because you did not complete the project."

"But I worked on that project for almost a month," he sputters.

"Yes, you did. But the bonus is for those who completed their portions of the project yesterday," you say evenly. "The bonus that would have been yours was used to pay the staffer who worked after hours last night to complete what you didn't."

That colleague opens his mouth and then closes it. He's stunned. Clearly there's nothing about your words he can argue with. He knows he frittered away his time yesterday and didn't complete that project. After a minute, he exhales. He meets your eyes and gives a single nod. He gets the message.

Do you think that colleague will pay more attention to his deadlines in the future? Will he be more responsible to complete his portion of projects? You be the judge.

Good disciplinary strategies allow individuals the free-dom to choose their actions. They also hold them accountable. But the Leman Way is unique in that it also stresses a *relational* connection. As leader, you respect the person while encourag-ing beneficial changes through real-life consequences. You don't lecture like an authoritarian. You don't enable like a permissive leader. Instead, you engineer an environment where the individual realizes, *I'll be money ahead if I get with the program and do what I'm supposed to do.*

How can you put relational discipline into play? Follow these seven principles.

### #1: Focus on the 3 Rs, not rules.

One of the broad themes in this book, as I noted earlier, is relationships. The 3 Rs are critical to leadership: **R**elationship, **R**elationship, **R**elationship. And yes, in case you're wondering, my repetition is *purposive.* See how useful that word is?

Relational discipline starts and ends with *you.* It only works if you have fostered a relationship with your colleagues. You have to know them, and they have to know you.

There's something else too. Take a closer look at the phrase "relational discipline." Did you notice that the word *relational* comes before the word *discipline?* There's a reason for that. Leadership is not about the rules. It's about having the right relationships. Without first having a relationship, rules mean nothing to those you serve and who serve with you.

### Thoughts of a Successful Leader

Rules without relationships lead to rebellion.

JOSH McDOWELL, EVANGELIST,
RELATIONAL TRAILBLAZER

Disciplinary interactions shouldn't be single transactions, like getting money out of an ATM. Instead, they should be *transformational.* Transformations occur when leaders keep in mind the ABCs (Acceptance, Belonging, and Competence), that relationships must come before rules, and that everything they do is part of bettering their colleagues and encouraging them to be lifelong learners.

### #2: Establish a healthy authority.

Authoritative leaders don't carry a big stick. They walk softly and confidently. They give authentic compliments about the positive attitude, virtues, and hard work ethic they see in others. They develop connections that pay off when things go well and not so well. When dealing with a detrimental behavior, great leaders keep the ball of authority in their court as long as possible. They only pass it as a last option to another person or department.

Most of all, they never engage in a public power struggle. They know they will always lose that battle because they have way more to lose than their colleague does. If you don't believe me, think for a minute. The last time you and a colleague locked horns, which of you hoped no one else heard or saw it? Likely it was you, and that doesn't bode well for your leadership. It's typically the more embarrassed one who gives in to the other's manipulation.

Your colleagues know who's in charge. If it's not you, it's them. If you aren't consistent, don't have clear procedures, and haven't crafted a roadmap for your work together, the most enterprising member will attempt to take control.

You can set all the rules you want for how colleagues *should* behave. But without relational discipline, there will be no long-lasting behavioral change.

> Your colleagues know who's in charge. If it's not you, it's them.

### #3: Let reality be the teacher.

True or False? The only way a person learns responsibility is by facing the consequences for his actions and being held accountable.

True.

Actions have consequences that can provide lasting lessons if the person is not rescued from them by a well-intentioned but controlling leader. Letting reality be the teacher means you allow a person's actions to naturally dictate what happens next. After all, isn't that what happens in real life?

If you don't set your alarm, you're late and have to explain why. If you're disorganized and don't get going on that task, you might have to miss break time to finish it. If you forget to bring your lunch, you might have to settle for vending machine snacks or the day-old coffee in the break room. If you start a war of words with a colleague, you still have to see her every day. Things might be rather icy until you choose to apologize.

Are those real-life situations uncomfortable? Of course. But if you don't allow others to experience the consequences of their choices, you short-circuit their learning. What individuals experience for themselves they're not likely to forget.

---

### LEMANISM #16
A healthy adult is not always a happy adult.

---

When you allow your colleagues to make choices, some will choose wisely. Others will choose poorly. Allowing reality to play out will boost decision-making skills, help them play well with others, and encourage them to contribute to their community. The sooner people learn responsibility and accountability, the better off they and everyone around them will be.

#### #4: Win your colleagues' cooperation.

How do you intentionally win cooperation? And what might that look like? Again, it starts with the 3 Rs. You must have a relationship. You must know others and understand them.

If you have more than a few colleagues or clients, this task might seem overwhelming. However, it only takes a few minutes each day. Greet those you serve and who serve with you. Show interest in what they are interested in. Treat them as people of value, not pawns on a chessboard, numbers, or sales invoices.

Take Michael, for example. He's the Managing Partner at a large law firm, heading up multiple divisions and over two dozen attorneys. *Busy* is an understated descriptor of his workday and responsibilities. However, when he arrives on Monday, he makes a point to go office to office with a short 1-minute personalized greeting.

To Joe: "How was the barbecue this weekend? Any good recipes I could try?"

To Carmen: "Did your daughter have her baby as you expected this weekend? Everything go okay?"

To Ansel: "How's the apartment hunting going?"

On Fridays he arrives with a tray of coffees and teas. Each week, on a revolving basis, he treats four attorneys to their favorite flavor. Now if you had a leader like that, who was also fair with his case assignment and available for questions and brainstorming, wouldn't you feel supported in your work? Appreciated as a person?

Michael treats his staff equally but never the same. He goes out of his way to celebrate their differences. His actions uphold his words, modeling that no one attorney is more important than another. All have specific roles to play and are empowered to play those roles with a leader who has their back.

Everyone deserves to be treated equally with respect and kindness. Do so, and you'll set yourself up well for handling conflict down the road. Relational discipline allows you to assume the sideline position of coach. You come alongside a colleague, retain her dignity, *and* win her cooperation in solving the issue. Now that's a win-win.

### Thoughts of a Successful Leader

Customers will never love a company
until the employees love it first.

SIMON SINEK, AUTHOR & SPEAKER

### #5: React, don't respond.

Nothing destroys the camaraderie of a work environment or interpersonal relationships faster than reacting instead of responding. Reacting is easy. Simply open your mouth and blurt out whatever is on your mind without thinking of the consequences.

Responding is harder. It requires discipline. It entails reining in your emotions and considering consequences before you speak and act. It means choosing not to fuel flare-ups or exacerbate negative behavior.

Fools rush in. Wise persons take measured steps. Great leaders think ahead. They form strategies to handle specific situations *before* they occur. Feelings aren't right or wrong. They're just feelings. You can be angry and still be good.

Don't know what to say in a heated moment? Try these words for starters:

- "Let me ponder that thought, and I'll get back to you…."

- "I could be wrong…."

- "I might be out in left field on this…."

- "I'd like to think that idea through…."

- "I don't have all the facts yet, but let's talk later today…."

- "I'd like to hear your perspective on…."

- "Tell me more about that…."

Such words allow you to gather the facts and clarify your thinking. They help you regroup after reactive thoughts such as, *That's the dumbest idea I've ever heard,* or *Why does he always create trouble?* Using such starting words models respect and caring.

After your timeout and assessment, realize that there are some people in life who need a wake-up call. They need to hear a straightforward perspective privately from a person they respect. Contrary to their opinion, they aren't the center of the universe. Others do matter.

> Feelings aren't right or wrong. They're just feelings. You can be angry and still be good.

Remember, one of your roles as leader is to assist people in bettering themselves. That includes you. When you blow your top, be the first to say these magic words: "I'm sorry. I was wrong. Please forgive me." As for others, take advantage of teachable moments when they're ready to listen. Then state words like these kindly: "When you did that, your colleagues might have interpreted that as you saying, 'I'm the only important one here.'" Such a response ought to give that person something to think about before his head hits the pillow.

### Thoughts of a Successful Leader

I am not a product of my circumstances.
I am a product of my decisions.

STEPHEN R. COVEY, AMERICAN EDUCATOR, BUSINESSMAN, AUTHOR

### #6: Let your actions match your words.

Consistency is critical. You must do what you say you'll do.

If you say, "I'll let you go this time, but don't let it happen again," what do you think speaks louder? The words "don't let it happen again" or the act of letting that person go?

What about "I guess you didn't hear my directions the first time, so I'll tell you again"? Which phrase speaks louder?

I could give more examples, but they would all have the same result. The action wins every time. If you want people to accept responsibility for their actions, you cannot let them off the hook. Always follow through on what you say you'll do.

> **Always follow through on what you say you'll do.**

And, by the way, telling anyone to do something more than once is disrespectful. What you're really saying is, "I don't trust you to do what I asked you to do, so I have to tell you twice. Then maybe you'll remember and actually do it."

Don't get on that twice-is-better track. Say it once. What that person chooses to do afterward is up to him. Let the consequences, beneficial or detrimental, rain down to match his actions.

---

**LEMANISM #17**

Say it once. Turn your back. And walk away.

---

### #7: Role-model the virtues and values you want to see.

Want your colleagues to be honest? Model honesty. Want them to be positive? The buck stops with you. Want them to be kind? Then be kind. Want them to value family? Engineer workloads to ensure they can make their kids' soccer games and be home for family dinners.

Want them to pursue excellence? Do the same in your work. But never, ever push the high bar of perfection because it's impossible to hit. Doing so only sets others up for a nasty fall and a harsh landing. Instead, be honest about the times you tried to hit that bar and failed. Amazingly, life as you knew it did not end that day. Yes, things were rough for a while, but eventually they turned out all right.

Such conversations give your colleagues permission and freedom to try new things, even if they don't succeed at first. They don't have to fear you'll be upset. They are free to research, explore boundaries you supply, and to view varying perspectives and possibilities.

There is little in life, other than death and taxes, that's a given. However, it's also a given that *you* are in charge of *you*. What core values will colleagues see in you? What virtues will you model?

## Work It Out

Imagine you are having private conversations with Molly, Jonas, and Rebecca, whose stories were shared at the beginning of this chapter. How would your perspective change if you discovered the following details? In light of the new facts, how might you assist them to be their best selves while accomplishing their work excellently?

*Hint: This is your opportunity to assemble what you've learned thus far as an authoritative leader who practices relational discipline.*

### Molly's Story

Molly, a middleborn, is a single parent. Her older parents live 20 minutes away in their own residence. Her siblings live in other states, so she's the go-to adult caretaker.

Last weekend, her mother fell and broke her hip. With one parent hospitalized and the other still at home, Molly has been helping out a lot. In the morning, she's at the hospital, visiting her mom and getting updates from doctors on early rounds.

After work, she picks up her two teenagers at a public library near their school, drops them off at home, and pops dinner in the microwave. Then she's off to take her dad to the hospital. While he visits his wife, Molly races back to his house to make meals and clean a little. She picks him up before visiting hours close.

When Molly gets home at 9:00 p.m., crawling into bed is the only thing on her mind. She feels torn between being a daughter and a mom. Her kids complain about her never being home. She's not sure of her options. Should she move her parents in with her permanently? But is that fair to her kids? After all, it's their home too.

Then there's work. She feels guilty for being late, but she's running ragged. She hates that she's distracted. She feels responsible for her work and the people there. She doesn't want to let anyone down. But how can she do it all? How can she live with all that weight without going under?

*What Would You Do?*

(Fill in the blank.)

## Jonas's Story

Jonas, an only child, grew up in a home with parents who tolerated no "tomfoolery," as his dad used to say. If Jonas was quiet and did what he was told, when he was told, all went well. If not, he was in big trouble. One tiny infraction and the "I'm disappointed in you, and you're grounded" speech descended.

His life has always been tightly controlled, first by his parents, and then by himself. They expected a lot of him. He was a little adult by age seven. Now as an actual adult, he expects even more out of himself.

Being alone is a routine, and he's comfortable with it. Others are unpredictable, like wildcards in a game he has no experience playing. Break times, per his evaluation, seem to require three things he's not good at: conversation, laughter, and camaraderie.

Jonas prefers his own company because he knows what to expect. Just like he knows exactly how the strawberry yogurt he eats at his desk every morning will taste. He buys the same yogurt brand every time at the same grocery store. It's another comfortable routine. He likes it when life is simple and streamlined.

*What Would You Do?*

(Fill in the blank.)

## Rebecca's Story

Rebecca, a firstborn, has a powerful drive to excel and leadership ability. Others look to her for advice, and she easily rallies followers. When she raised the question, five other people in the meeting nodded, as if they'd like to know the answer to that question too.

Rebecca is highly detailed. Critical thinking comes naturally. She's spent enough time at your workplace that she's antsy to expand her knowledge and influence. She feels stuck. She has eagle-eyed some processes that could be streamlined and improved to benefit her colleagues and boost the company's bottom line.

However, in her current position, she feels powerless. Why would upper management listen to her? She'd love the opportunity to expand her responsibilities but doesn't know how to go about such a move or if it would be welcomed. That long-held-back internal tension prompted her rather in-your-face question in the meeting.

*What Would You Do?*

(Fill in the blank.)

## It's Your Turn in the Driver's Seat

Did you know that Formula One cars are the fastest regulated racing cars in the world? Each F1 team builds its own car with front and rear wings to assist in cornering on a track in high speeds. To satisfy racing rules, that car must have operable reverse gears. But because an F1 driver uses that gear so rarely, the reverse mechanism is usually kept as small and light as possible. Once a driver gets behind the wheel, it is very difficult to go in reverse.

The same is true of leadership. Once your leadership car is going down a particular track of authoritarianism or permissiveness, it can be difficult to reverse that motion. However, it's not impossible. As a leader friend used to say, "Impossible is an opinion. Not a fact. For every crisis, there's an opportunity to rethink your strategy and do things differently."

This book is your opportunity to evaluate your current strategies. So sit in that driver's seat right now. What's working? What's not working? How might you do things differently to get you toward your goal of being a great leader by Friday?

When you understand that behavior is purposive, win your colleagues' cooperation, and use relational discipline, you'll be set up well for your laps around the work track. Combine that with intentionally crafting your own unique culture, the subject of the next chapter, and you and your team will be cheering together at the finish line.

## Winning Play #5
## Craft Your Own Unique, Intentional Culture

*Know, communicate, and role-model your why.*

Imagine right now that you're walking into the foyer of a company. What clues would you see as to its culture? Its vision and how that vision is carried out? If you were there for an interview to assist in expanding their work, how might you address that existing culture you see and feel in a positive light? How might you encourage that company to broaden its vision in a way that you might participate in its growth?

Five years ago Amelia was in that position. Upon entering a decades-old company, it took only a minute's observation to get the lay of the land. The foyer was eerily silent other than her footsteps' echo on the tiled floor. Heavy leather chairs lined the dark wood walls. The receptionist's head was barely visible above the looming desk, empty except for a bronze vintage call bell. A large wall plaque proclaimed "Hard Work and Excellence Lead to Success" with a "#1 in the Industry for 20 years" underneath.

Such a landscape might have been intimidating. But Amelia was a dynamic, gutsy leader who had already assisted two other companies in reinventing themselves and powering ahead. She understood that even a #1 company should not rest on its laurels. She had done extensive research, grappled with each company's vision, and evaluated its successes and failures. Then, despite their reticence to change, she had nudged them step by step into clarifying and expanding their original vision by showing them how it could be done in her department. Once those companies saw proof that good things came from change, they got on board enthusiastically with the progress and considered options for other departments.

The results were stellar. The board and investors were pleased with the improved financial picture. New products expanded the company's reach and infused energy into quarterly meetings. Forward-thinking strategy allowed the leaders to adhere to their founding mission yet push the envelope and boost their reputation in the industry.

Long story short, Amelia was hired at the stodgy company, despite some skepticism and grumbling about her newfangled ideas. Within a year, her department was not only the top performer with the highest sales and profit margin but had created a new product that was selling like hotcakes. Colleagues who had raised eyebrows at the way she managed her division got curious about the why of her success.

Visitors began to poke their heads in the door. As they cautiously entered, their responses were almost comical. They would pause in awe as if entering a completely different world... and it was.

### *Thoughts of a Successful Leader*

Culture is like the wind. It is invisible;
yet its effect can be seen and felt.

BRYAN WALKER, PARTNER AND MANAGING DIRECTOR, IDEO

Amelia had transformed the sterile white walls of the main gathering area into a vibrantly colored, energetic environment of scattered small tables and leafy plants. Inspiring quotes were painted here and there on the walls in oranges, reds, blues, and greens. The company motto was featured in a large, avant-garde style on one wall. Four large wall-mounted whiteboards presented evolving questions that colleagues scribbled on as they passed by to get coffee and tea at the nearby station.

That wcck's questions:

- "What is excellence?"

- "What is success?"

- "How could we do what we are doing…but better?"

- "Your craziest idea that just might work…"

One might think such a culture would be a loud free-for-all. However, it was amazingly quiet and productive. Small offices of hard-at-work colleagues ringed the main area. Their doors opened for scheduled in-person meetings, and at 10:00 a.m., 12:00 noon, and 3:00 p.m. for half-hour breaks. Amelia had listened to her team who wanted three half-hour brain breaks, rather than the traditional two 15-minute breaks and hour lunch the rest of the company had.

During those breaks, colleagues snacked, chatted, or had a walkabout for exercise. Amelia joined them on Fridays at noon for light-hearted discussions. One led to her installing "The Exchange," a cork board where colleagues could post intriguing articles, memes, or questions like, "What's your favorite antique store within 20 miles of here?" or "Anybody got a tent I could borrow for the weekend?"

When breaks were over, those people didn't need reminders to get back to work. They cared about their jobs because Amelia cared about them. She listened to them, provided the interaction they needed to gel as a team, and encouraged personal bests. They knew they were accepted by the group, belonged to the group, and that Amelia considered their contributions valuable. Finally, she not only *allowed* but *provided* time and space for fun and joined it.

Amelia's department became known for its hard-work ethic, passion for excellence, and groundbreaking products that far exceeded expectations. She did it by fulfilling the original vision "Hard Work and Excellence Lead to Success" in her own unique way.

How about you? If you could start from scratch and create a win-win environment, what would it look like? A culture where all would:

- Treat each other with respect, honesty, integrity, and kindness.

- Appreciate, support, and celebrate differences.

- Handle problems and disagreements swiftly, fairly, and without drama.

- Listen attentively.

- Eagerly participate in discussions.

- Partner to perform tasks with enthusiasm and without prompting or complaining.

- Intentionally view life from behind each others' eyes.

- Do what they say they will do, when they say they will do it.

- Fill in the blank with more of your ideas.

What would also represent your flair and showcase what matters most to you? If you are part of a larger company, crafting your own space doesn't mean you don't adhere to that company's vision and rules. You do so with excellence like Amelia did. But when others step into your corner, they see and feel your spin.

> If you could start from scratch and create a win-win environment, what would it look like?

To craft your own culture you need to be intentional. You need to plan. Have you compiled your thoughts into a purpose statement you read frequently to remind you what you're doing and why you're doing it? Have you communicated that why to those you serve and who serve with you?

If you have, I applaud you. You're about 1% of the population. The other 99% of us really need this chapter. It will show you how to identify, communicate, and model your why to create the culture you desire. It will introduce you to the 5 Ps of Partnership to help you become the effective leader you long to be. Better yet, as you establish a growth mindset, you can use principles you learn in any arena you inhabit. What's not to like about that?

### Finding Your Why

Why are you doing what you're doing? Is it just a job or a joy? Is it only a project or a passion? Are you simply putting in time, or are you excited about being a difference-maker? Are you driven to excel because you see the benefits for others?

Leaders who create intentional environments identify their why and use that why to its fullest potential. They know their why and refine it as skills and knowledge expand. They rehearse their why so they can easily communicate it to colleagues, clients, or anyone who asks. They consistently model their why. What does that look like?

### *Know your why.*

If you're looking for a job, you should make sure you know the mission of that company before you walk through that door. Otherwise, it won't take long for them to figure out that you're punting and don't know what you're talking about.

What about if you're already in that job? Individuals often pay attention to a company's vision while in the hiring process. But unless leaders regularly refer to that vision and how it applies to current decisions and projects, it's easy for colleagues to forget why they are doing what they're doing and how their puzzle piece fits into the whole.

The same goes for pro-bono and community work. Unless that group has a vision statement, refers to it, and adheres to it, that collection of individuals won't get anywhere for long. They'll get distracted and teeter off course.

What about your home environment? Have you crafted a vision statement? Is it displayed prominently where everyone who lives there can see it? Brooklyn, a mom of four growing boys, posts hers on the busiest place in her house: the refrigerator door. Ahni and his four-year-old made a crayon masterpiece that hangs above her toy basket. Alonzo and his housemates hang theirs on the entry door from the garage to the kitchen.

A vision statement includes your core values, virtues you want to uphold, how you will view, treat, and serve others, and other elements that make your culture unique. When my five kids were young, we had numerous discussions about values, virtues, and how to treat others. So many in fact, that when they were older, all I had to say when they went out the door was, "Remember, you're a Leman." That short phrase was a kindly reminder that they were representatives of our unique family culture in all that they said and did.

Without a vision statement, your boat will be rudderless on the ocean of life. That's because such a statement emphasizes what matters most. It provides a roadmap for where you are going and how you are getting there together. It gives guidelines for handling disagreements and provides acceptable problem-solving routes. It encapsulates your end goal.

> A vision statement includes your core values, virtues you want to uphold, how you will view, treat, and serve others, and other elements that make your culture unique.

One of the best condensed vision statements I've seen is this one:

> We are a safe, invigorating, we're-all-in-this-together-attitude community that works together, plays together, problem-solves together, listens attentively to each other, acts with kindness, respect, and caring, and supports and applauds each other as we discover, develop, and pursue excellence in our unique arenas.

This statement could apply to *any* arena, couldn't it? My thanks to the friend who graciously supplied it for this book and whose family has lived it out for the nearly three decades I've known them.

### Thoughts of a Successful Leader

The reason most people never reach their goals is that they don't define them, or ever seriously consider them as believable or achievable. Winners can tell you where they are going, what they plan to do along the way, and who will be sharing the adventure with them.

DENIS WAITLEY, AMERICAN WRITER AND MOTIVATIONAL SPEAKER

### Communicate your why.

Now that you know your vision, the next step is to share that vision with those who serve with you. A first step is to post it where all can see it. Next is breaking that statement down into bite-sized chunks and explaining why each is important to the group's goals. Colleagues need to walk away knowing the purpose of the group and how it will go about fulfilling that purpose.

If you are considering leadership or at the beginning of your opportunity, you can start out on the right foot in a brand-new shoe rather than one that may need some repairs. For those who have been leaders for years, it's never too late to polish that scuffed toe or fix that broken-down heel. In fact, today is a good day to start.

Hal worked with people who wouldn't typically inhabit the same circles, so he chose to be proactive. First he explained the group's purpose. Next he clarified why each aspect of their vision statement mattered and contributed to the culture he wanted to build. Then he got busy winning his new colleagues' cooperation.

"Every person in this room is here for a reason," he told the group. "I hand-picked each of you because you excel at what you do and have a track record for being a team player." He gave each participant a well-deserved introduction and brief spotlight to show his appreciation and support. That's because he knew that authentic compliments and belief in a person can knock down walls of differences and open doors of communication.

> Authentic compliments and belief in a person can knock down walls of differences and open doors of communication.

He closed the time with this encouragement: "I believe in each of you, and in what we can do together. In three months, I have no doubt we'll look back at this moment and say, 'That was the start of something beautiful.' So let's get to it, shall we?"

I've said it earlier, but I'll say it again: "Expect the best, and you'll likely get the best." Choose a positive set-up, major on relationships, and I guarantee you'll be on your way to the successful completion of that project.

Communicating your why isn't a one-time affair, though. Your colleagues will need reminders of what they are working for. Little check-ins and celebrations of passed milestones assist with keeping motivation high. Acknowledging wins privately and publicly giving credit where credit is due will increase your colleagues' buy-in. In short, you must be the continuing inspiration they seek.

### Thoughts of a Successful Leader

Motivation is everything. You can do the work
of two people, but you can't be two people.
Instead, you have to inspire the next guy down the line
and get him to inspire his people.

LEE IACOCCA, AMERICAN BUSINESSMAN, FORD MOTOR COMPANY,
CHRYSLER CORPORATION

### Role-model your why.

Ed, a construction superintendent, is on a tight budget. His company pays for only one group meal on location a year. With three kids at home, Ed isn't rolling in money either. But Ed has found a creative way to engage regularly with his coworkers and foster conversation and problem-solving.

The first Monday of every month he arrives loaded with a tray of treats he bakes himself over the weekend. He sets up a small grouping of chairs to the side where he can welcome one-on-one or small-group discussion. His coworkers spend their first 10 minutes of the morning enjoying the goodies and conversation.

On the last Monday of every month, Ed takes them all for a rapid walk-through of the building they're working on. As they see the progress of individual teams and become aware of how significant each of their roles is in the overall project, the workers are spurred on to excellence. As a bonus, the four workers who tended to be late on Monday mornings now arrive on time. They don't want to miss the treats, the camaraderie, or the walk-through.

## Work It Out

### Dos and Don'ts for Relational Connection

*Dos:*

1. Say, "I'd love to hear what you do for fun."
2. Use "Tell me more about that" to learn more information.
3. Briefly contribute your own experiences that relate to hobbies and interests.
4. Give all who want to share a little slice of talking time.

*Don'ts:*

1. Ask questions.
2. Focus on work.
3. Talk to fill the space…especially about yourself.
4. Pressure anyone to talk. This is the *opportunity* to connect, not interrogation.

What is Ed intentionally doing? He's role-modeling his why. He knows that his workers, scattered across the large building, don't usually have much interaction as a group. He also knows that some might lack motivation if they don't feel their work is important. The Boss is known for his hard work, fairness in disputes, respectful attitude, and kind but straightforward interactions. He's not only available but makes it easy for coworkers to connect with him.

### Thoughts of a Successful Leader

Determine what behaviors and beliefs you value
as a company, and have everyone live true to them.
These behaviors and beliefs should be so essential
to your core that you don't even think of it as culture.

BRITTANY FORSYTH, SVP OF HR, SHOPIFY

Great leaders model their why in their values and relationships. When you set aside regular times for colleagues to talk with you one-on-one or as part of a group, the rewards will be immense. You will get to know them, and they will get to know you. Down the road those relationships will allow you to handle intense situations admirably for a better outcome. That's why, if you remember only two things I tell you in this book, let it be these: Live by your values, and never forget the 3 Rs.

# Indicators of an Ineffective Leader

1. The environment feels cold and sterile, like a doctor's office.

2. Colleagues are stressed, fearful, and won't take risks due to an authoritarian leader.

3. The workplace is disorganized, lacks clear procedures, and feels like a free-for-all zone.

4. Colleagues assume leadership due to the permissive leader's default.

5. The leader repeats instructions, cajoles or threatens to get tasks done, and doesn't complete his own work.

6. Colleagues drag their feet starting on projects and dilly-dally to extend break times.

7. They look bored or tuned out and talk to neighbors when the leader speaks.

8. The leader always addresses the whole group rather than connecting with individuals.

# Indicators of Effective Leadership

1. The environment has a warm, energetic, positive, and organized vibe.

2. The authoritative leader demonstrates healthy control and support in a conducive-to-working-and-learning environment.

3. The leader manages his time and materials to meet deadlines, provides a roadmap, gives clear instructions, and trusts colleagues to follow them.

4. Colleagues respond immediately and respectfully to leader requests.

5. Colleagues happily contribute ideas, and the leader makes the final call on which ones to pursue.

6. All in the group are purposefully engaged in the work and invested in it.

7. The leader is consistent in speech and actions, doing what he says he will do.

8. The leader models respect and an authentic connection with each team member.

Great leaders know that people tend to emulate what they see. That's why great leaders hold themselves to the highest standards. They role-model their why through their attitude, the virtues they display, and the service they provide.

*Attitude.* While on a flight a few years ago, I sat across the aisle from a senior executive of a large firm. Being a lastborn and innately curious, I introduced myself and struck up a conversation. "From what I've seen, making a profit in your industry is no small challenge."

He nodded. "We're constantly trying to find ways to reduce costs. That includes making changes in the number of employees we have and how we pay them." He sighed. "Not always popular decisions. Most of the senior business leaders I know would much prefer to avoid decisions that create hardship for individual employees. I am one of those. But we always have to balance that penchant with making a profit. Without profit, the long-term outlook for those employees would be very bad. So I'm always looking for new ways to protect their interests *and* simultaneously grow the company."

That's the attitude of a leader. That senior executive didn't sugarcoat the very real problems and challenges. He was honest about the difficulty of walking a fine line between being popular with employees and making a profit to ensure the company's viability. He pursued excellence, didn't give up in the midst of challenges, and had a learning-for-a-lifetime attitude.

What is your attitude toward your work? Toward those who work with you? Do you pursue excellence or adopt "just good enough to get the job done" thinking? Your answers to those questions greatly impact the quality of your work, showcase your personal values, and influence how you relate to others.

*Virtues.* What is written on the tablet of a leader's heart will determine his success or failure in the long run. Richard Nixon was a superb negotiator. Bill Clinton boosted the American economy. But both failed morally and are remembered for those failures.

---

**LEMANISM #18**

An environment is always defined
by the lowest accepted behavior.

---

What virtues are important to you? Integrity? If you don't have integrity, you'll find it difficult someday to face yourself in the mirror. Honesty? It *is* always the best policy. As Judge Judy Sheindlin once quipped, "If you tell the truth, then you don't have to have a good memory." Self-control? Responding rather than reacting is the only way to fly without crash-landing. Humility? You can't get to where you are now or where you want to be someday without others' partnership. Leaders never act like a one-person show. They know they are stronger as part of a team.

The change you'd like to see in your environment starts with you. Why not inspire others to be better by being better yourself? Holding yourself to the highest standards is fully within your control.

### *Thoughts of a Successful Leader*

Why is culture so important to a business?
Here is a simple way to frame it.
The stronger the culture,
the less corporate process a company needs.
When the culture is strong,
you can trust everyone to do the right thing.
BRIAN CHESKY, CO-FOUNDER AND CEO, AIRBNB

*Service.* What is your view of those you serve, those who serve with you, and how they should be treated? Are they merely the means to an end of accomplishing the job? Or do you want to get to know them? To serve them in ways that encourage, support, and empower them? What does that look like?

Shanna, the director of an art department, had a large center office with doors on three sides. Though her space was a thoroughfare of traffic and conversation, her staff complained they didn't have break space or enough access to her. She wanted to be open to creative conversation, but she was overwhelmed by it and unable to get her work done.

It was time to instill order to the chaos. She posted two questions on a confidential online poll: *How would you improve break times? How could I make it easier for you to connect with me?* By afternoon, she had a plethora of honest answers.

The following morning, in an all-staff meeting in the break room, she scanned the group. Her colleagues were right. The room *was* much too small to accommodate them all. After thanking them for their feedback, she explained the goals and details of their surprise group project from 3:30-4:30 p.m. that afternoon. They would repurpose the department space in a way that made sense for their needs.

In a single hour at the end of a Friday, when colleagues were often demotivated, a transformation took place. The three-door thoroughfare office became the new break/lunchroom. Shanna's office was newly housed in the former break/lunchroom. To celebrate the moves, the enterprising art intern made a welcome sign for Shanna's office: COME ON IN! WED + FRI 3:30-4:30 P.M. The break room's schedule listed specific windows for meetings, breaks, and lunches.

Fast forward three months. Running that poll and spending a single hour had indeed reinvented their workplace. Colleagues had taken personal interest by adding decorations, extra chairs, and spare tables. They took breaks together. The space could now house the entire group for lunch. Smiles and laughs abounded.

Shanna was also getting her work done. During her two "office hours" a week, she welcomed individuals, small groups, and discussion on any topic. Work satisfaction in her department soared. After the first two months, she had condensed her office hours to a single hour time slot on Friday and scheduled Small Group Brainstorms the other hour. She varied attendees to keep discussions lively and provide fresh perspectives. Colleagues interacted much more naturally because they knew each other better. She had fewer staff scuffles to solve.

Shanna could have pulled out the almighty authoritarian card. She could have said, "This constant walking back and forth in my office has to stop. From now on, my doors are shut. If you want my attention, email me. I'll respond when I can."

She could have rolled over with permissiveness and put up with the interruptions and tromping back and forth. She could have kept her complaints internal: *Well, I guess they'll do what they do. There's nothing much I can do about it.*

Instead, she acted as a leader with healthy authority. She asked for her colleagues' thoughts in a way that would not put them on the spot. She evaluated their ideas and settled on one that was time-efficient, financially savvy (free), and would solve both issues. In the meeting, she thanked them for their input, briefly explained her decision, and respectfully asked for their assistance in carrying out that transformation.

Great leaders make it easy for others to connect with them. They desire to know those they serve and who serve with them. They go out of their way to show others how much they care. They identify needs, rally others for solutions, and then make an authoritative decision, followed by action steps.

What is the biggest problem you need to solve right now? How might you move forward on that issue? The time you spend positively engaging with and serving colleagues will pay off in huge dividends. For starters, it's far better than sitting in meetings with angry colleagues who feel you have taken advantage of them or don't appreciate their work.

## The 5 Ps of Partnership

> The time you spend positively engaging with and serving colleagues will pay off in huge dividends.

Great leaders use what I call "The 5 Ps of Partnership." Their interactions are **P**urposeful, **P**ersistent, **P**ositive, **P**rofessional, and **P**roactive. Use them, and they'll not only help you start out right but will keep you trucking down the road even when bumps arise.

### Be Purposeful

If you don't know where you are going, how can you get there? We already talked about knowing, communicating, and role-modeling the why of your vision. But great leaders also accomplish what they set out to do. They start *and* finish well. Sure, they face obstacles along the way, but they are not sidetracked.

Many so-called leaders are great starters but poor finishers. They have ideas galore, but no willpower to follow through for the long haul. They stall in the middle and don't bring their ideas to fruition.

Great leaders set their compass and don't deviate from the path. Yes, a strong wind might knock them off into the weeds every once in a while. But they get up, dust themselves off, and step back on that path. They are driven by their vision to complete what they started.

### Thoughts of a Successful Leader

If you are working on something that you really care about, you don't have to be pushed. The vision pulls you.

STEVE JOBS, AMERICAN BUSINESSMAN, COFOUNDER OF APPLE INC.

Purposeful leaders are intentional. They set an atmosphere where colleagues are routinely informed and have the opportunity to invest in the work. They set high standards and expectations and model them. They display beneficial attitudes, live out their values and virtues, and liberally use the 7 Essential Vitamins. They work to understand their colleagues, support them, and advocate for them. They provide what people desire most: the ABCs of Acceptance, Belonging, and Competence.

### Be Persistent

During the early days of World War II, when Britain and France were the only allied countries fighting against Hitler's rise in Europe and Africa, statesman Winston Churchill became the British Prime Minister. On October 29, 1941, four months after Germany invaded the Soviet Union,[27] Churchill showed up at his former alma mater, Harrow School, in northwest London. In the midst of catastrophic world events, he spoke these inspiring, empowering words: "Never give in, never give in, never, never, never, never in nothing, great or small, large or petty…Never yield to force…we have only to persevere to conquer."[28]

When you're a leader, things won't always go well or by the book. That's the bad news.

But here's the good news. If you expect such to occur, you won't be surprised or dismayed. It's always within your power to *respond* to circumstances. Your duty when confronting any challenge is to never give in. Keep your sight on that end goal. Review your plans. Make adjustments in your steps where needed. Then take baby steps toward that goal until you can run toward it like a champion athlete. Good things come to those who are patient and tenacious in their pursuit.

## *Thoughts of a Successful Leader*

The difference between the impossible
and the possible lies in a person's determination.

Tommy Lasorda, American Baseball Manager

### *Be Positive*

Ever hear the folksy saying, "You can catch more flies with honey than with vinegar?" It's true. People will flock around a positive person while they will run from a negative person.

Choosing to be positive is a leadership strategy that has exponential relational dividends. Never underestimate the power of positive expectations. It is healthy and good to have high expectations and to state those in a positive way regularly to your colleagues.

Never underestimate the value of sincere encouragement or your belief in another person either. Be a champion and a cheerleader. You may be the only one who provides such rarities in that person's life. You already know that all of us crave attention. Wouldn't you rather give others attention for positive actions than allow them the opportunity to dream up some negative ones to make you pay attention?

Here's a simple solution that's easy to implement. Why not make it a personal goal to share one positive thing you observe about a colleague each week? The hunt will keep you energized. It will sharpen your awareness of all that is going on in your environment.

> Never underestimate the value of sincere encouragement.

Communicating positively also lessens the probability of issues cropping up. Your relationship is already established. Handling problems can happen more easily and naturally. It's acceptable and right to let people know when you are disappointed in their behavior or performance. But you must always keep the power of positive expectations at the forefront of your discussions. Never focus on the *person* as "bad." Focus on the *actions* that were detrimental rather than beneficial. Minimize friction by stating in an even-keeled manner that you expect more because you believe they can do better.

---

**LEMANISM #19**

The power of positive expectations changes your conversation.

---

As an authoritative leader, you place the decision whether to do better or not in that colleague's court along with the real-life consequences. You offer your assistance and support in moving ahead in a positive direction. You clarify that, from your perspective, you are all on the same team. Win or lose, you do it together.

It takes only about 90 seconds to say something nice. Yet that statement will have a long-lasting legacy. It will color that individual's day with a rosier palette and emerge as a splash of sunshine on a cloudy day when he or she needs it most.

So stop by that desk and give a smile. Send or drop off an encouraging handwritten note. Leave a brief phone message to celebrate a milestone event. Say thank you to the colleague who quietly comes in every day and consistently works hard. Give a friendly wave to a customer when they leave.

There's a perk for you too. What goes around comes around. When you encourage someone else, you brighten up your own day as well.

### Be Professional

My college baseball coach once said to me, "Leman, if you can't play third base, at least look like you can. Tuck your shirt in." He was quite the encouraging mentor, but he did have a point.

You should do everything you can to appear professional. That means doing your homework before meetings and dressing appropriately and neatly.

Being professional also has to do with the words and gestures you choose to use, how you greet people, the tone of your communications, and so much more. When you are professional and relational, people are much more likely to take you seriously and think you can get the work done well.

> When you are professional and relational, people are much more likely to take you seriously and think you can get the work done well.

### Be Proactive

Some of the best overall advice for becoming a great leader by Friday can be stated in two words: "Be proactive." Everything we've explored in this book is set on that foundation.

On Monday, you learned how to get on the front end of maximizing your strengths. On Tuesday, you fine-tuned your leadership traits. On Wednesday you learned how to better understand how to serve those you serve. On Thursday you discovered one of the most important strategies of all: how to win cooperation. Friday has been all about being proactive in identifying, communicating, and role-modeling your why so you can craft your unique culture.

### Thoughts of a Successful Leader

You've got to get up every morning with determination if you're going to go to bed with satisfaction.

GEORGE LORIMER, AMERICAN JOURNALIST, EDITOR,
*THE SATURDAY EVENING POST*

Choosing to be proactive means you provide a roadmap of your purpose and goals. You decide how you will view and relate to your colleagues and customers. You set expectations up front, so all have the opportunity to hear your intentions and don't have to second-guess them.

---

**LEMANISM #20**

To get somewhere
you need a destination and a plan.

---

You post schedules and deadlines where all can view them. You stay organized. You start and end meetings on time. You manage your physical space to reflect the culture you want to have.

You are welcoming and accessible. You choose to respond rather than react. You decide to use relational discipline, allowing real-life consequences to play out. You wait for that teachable moment.

Instead of being defensive or offensive, you choose to listen. You calmly get the facts, assess the situation, and address potential solutions. You support others in their roles, but you don't do their work for them.

You give others your full attention when they talk with you. You communicate the information they need. You follow up on concerns or questions when you say you will.

You set the foundation for a respectful community with the 5 Ps.

Above all, you major on the 3 Rs.

## Work It Out

For each scenario, think of a "5 P" solution: **P**urposeful, **P**ersistent, **P**ositive, **P**rofessional, and **P**roactive. For additional perspective and ideas, brainstorm with another leader.

*Scenario #1:* A colleague seems to be avoiding you. He missed the last all-group meeting.

*Scenario #2:* Several individuals have shared information with you about a single employee. Their perspectives, though, seem to conflict.

*Scenario #3:* A customer calls. He's irate about a product he purchased and the service your company has provided.

*Scenario #4:* A colleague has struggled with her job responsibilities since the company merger. Lately, though, you see improvement.

███████████████████████████████████████

Powerful transformation can take place when you are **P**urposeful, **P**ersistent, **P**ositive, **P**rofessional, and **P**roactive.

- **P**urposeful in your goals, plans, and action steps.

- **P**ersistent in how you pursue and refine strategies and never give in.

- **P**ositive in your expectations, actions, and words.

- **P**rofessional in how you present yourself and interact.

- **P**roactive in all things.

Pair those 5 Ps with the 3 Rs and a Growth Mindset, and you've got a winning combination for success.

## A Growth Mindset

In Arizona we have an amazing plant called the saguaro. It's the largest type of cactus in the United States with a long life span. With care, at 70 years old it can be around six feet tall. Its first branch doesn't appear until it's at least 75, and it's not considered an adult until it's about 125.[29] It can tolerate drought and significant storms. But ignore any root rot, and that mighty saguaro can topple quickly.

The tale of the mighty saguaro is a good reminder for leaders. Intentionally setting up your unique culture is important to its long-term success. However, you must also carefully watch over and tend to that culture or root rot might creep in despite your best intentions. The tone you set is critical to establishing a respectful partnership. All values, virtues, attitudes, and your view of service start from you and spread out from there.

That means *you* are the difference-maker. No one else will do. *You* are the one who intentionally creates an environment that not only advances the work you do together but also gives colleagues the opportunity to grow.

Yes, sometimes it's quite the juggling act. But great leaders choose a growth mindset. That means you choose to be a lifelong learner. You are intensely curious. You admit you don't know everything. You read books to further your skills, attend workshops, and seek out mentors to provide fresh ideas and help you grow. You adapt to new information and embrace challenges. You regularly reflect on what you are learning.

You are also approachable. You invite suggestions from others and welcome questions. You comfortably share struggles and failures. You freely share resources and success tips to assist others.

You use an authoritative style rather than an authoritarian or permissive one. You gather the facts before you act. You evaluate options, make decisions even when they're hard, and adhere to them unless there is a logical reason to change course. You give credit where credit is due and never pass the buck of blame. You accept responsibility for your decisions.

You also know your why and go out of your way to communicate and role-model it. You treat every person with equal respect, kindness, and appreciation. You feel a deep responsibility for the role you play in others' lives. You are called to be where you are right now despite any current challenges that keep you up at night.

All those descriptors are true of a great leader. Great leaders aren't perfect. They're learners in progress. Think about where you were when you started this book on Monday. In only five days, look how far you've come already. That deserves a pat on the back, so give yourself one right now.

But you don't have to stop here. You can continue using the five winning plays to prepare and energize you for a positive impact wherever you roam. Imagine where you could be a month from now...a year from now...five years from now....

So get out those sparklers.

Celebrate your world-changing potential.

Let the party begin.

## Decide Your Legacy

*All of us will leave an imprint.*
*What will yours be?*

I once tracked down CEO Harvey Mackay, author of best-seller *Swim with the Sharks without Being Eaten Alive*, to interview him in person about the values of a business leader. He was known for making opportunities happen while operating with purpose and integrity. I wanted to know about the meaningful things that leaders care about even more than the bottom line and how they put those intangibles into practice.

Little did I know that Mackay would be between planes, "on top of a tiger" as he said kindly, when we caught up. He'd just spent six weeks free of charge pulling together a $125-million deal to keep the Minnesota Timberwolves in Minneapolis instead of moving to New Orleans. One might think that he could give his work for free since he was successful enough that he didn't need to be paid for that job. Or perhaps it was because he liked basketball or Minneapolis-St. Paul housed his corporation.

Instead, Mackay was focused on the intangibles of that work: helping others feel recognized and respected because of his concern and service. Mackay knew how valuable a pro franchise could be to the Twin Cities. He believed that fostering a spirit of loyalty and pride not only boosted relationships but would eventually lead to a better economy and living conditions for all. In short, Mackay wanted *everyone* in Minneapolis-St. Paul to be a winner.

What are you doing right now to ensure that everyone who comes in contact with you is a winner? Leadership isn't a one-and-done deal. It's about bettering yourself for a lifetime. It's also about changing others' lifetimes by assisting them as they develop into their best selves.

> What are you doing right now to ensure that everyone who comes in contact with you is a winner?

Every person on planet Earth will leave an imprint. It's impossible to be neutral. What legacy do you want to leave? Will you be the leader a colleague remembers years later? Who won her cooperation and motivated her during a difficult time? The leader who believed in his potential and took the risk of including him? The one who saw her developing skills and mentored her when others didn't consider her hirable? The leader who swept into a company and changed it from a toxic culture into a beneficial-for-all one?

Earlier in this book I asked how you hoped to be remembered. But what specifically would you want others to say about you, your accomplishments, and your relationships as a eulogy? I'll close our time together with five actions that will help you craft the unique legacy you dream of.

### #1: Align your priorities to what matters most.

If I asked you right now, "What are the three most important things in the world to you?" what would you say? Reflect for a few minutes. Then write those three things down.

*Don't worry. I'll wait right here until you're done....*

Now you're ready for the next step. Look at your schedule for next week. Does the time you've slotted to spend on projects and with people align with your top three priorities?

If so, you're one of the exceedingly rare people in this world. You have never once wavered from your convictions. You aren't sidetracked by any detours or curveballs thrown at you. You're always targeted in your interactions and focused on your goals.

If not, today's your day. It's within your power to start changing that schedule to adhere to your priorities. You can do it even if you have to work the same amount of hours.

How is that possible? When you know what matters most to you, and you live according to that creed, it's much easier to prioritize a constantly evolving to-do list. You intently focus while at work, keeping distractions to a minimum. You stick to agendas at scheduled meetings to make the best use of your time, others' time, and company resources. You take advantage of your short breaks during your work day to touch base with those most important to you or handle a small task you'd otherwise have to do on the way home or at home.

You show up on time for family dinners. You listen closely to your partner, communicate fully, and pay attention to what matters most to him or her. You are present, as much as humanly possible, to read the kids a bedtime story and tuck them into bed. You check on your older parents daily and have a meal with them once a week even though it's an hour drive to reach them. You show up with a surprise to cheer a friend experiencing a tough time.

> When you know what matters most to you, and you live according to that creed, it's much easier to prioritize a constantly evolving to-do list.

On occasion, when extra hours are required to complete a project, you step up to the plate. But you also do your best to explain it to those important to you, so they feel included in your work life. You plan a celebration with those people to mark the project's end and follow through with it.

Now look again at the three priorities you listed and your schedule for the week. Which tasks could you pass to someone else? Which tasks are no longer important compared to what matters most and could be moved to the "if I ever have time" category? Prune ruthlessly, and I bet you'll be surprised at the time that remains to do what matters most.

### #2: Be good and balanced.

Do you ever feel all stressed up, and you still have everyplace to go? Life is a conveyor belt. Sometimes that belt speeds up. Sometimes it slows down. And sometimes it moves along at a predictable pace. There are things you don't have control over, such as getting the flu. Others are your choice, such as deciding whether or not to travel to see your grandmother for her 75th birthday or taking on a second job to buy that new car instead of a used one.

Too much of anything is not a good thing. Busy is not necessarily better unless you are busy doing the things that matter. If you want to be successful as a leader in the long haul, you need to be balanced and take care of yourself. Set healthy routines for your body and mind and commit yourself to them.

### Thoughts of a Successful Leader

Do or do not. There is no try.
YODA IN STAR WARS: THE EMPIRE STRIKES BACK

Eat food that's good for you in appropriate quantities. Sure, you'll slip every once in a while and have a binge on those delicacies you love, but give healthy eating your best shot. I myself have been known in the past to eat an entire lemon meringue pie, slice by slice, in a single day. But now that I'm older, a bit heftier, and much wiser, I've changed that habit. My firstborn wife has also assisted in that regard by hiding the pie where I can't find it in the refrigerator.

A little exercise is also important to maintaining physical, mental, and emotional balance. The more simple the routine, the easier it will be to do it. It could be a morning jog at 5 a.m. with Fido, the family dog who appreciates the exercise and companionship. If you're an only or a firstborn, a short private walk around a nearby park during lunch could double as a clear-the-mental-fog time. If you're a middleborn or a lastborn, you might want to gather several colleagues for a chat-and-walk fest. Or if you're a more active sort not opposed to sweating, try an informal game of basketball in a neighbor's driveway once a week to relive those days of your youth. Your imagination is the limit.

It also helps to regularly get some sleep. If you are a night owl, don't also try to be an early morning bird. Pick one or the other and stick to the routine. All those things you feel like you have to get done? They'll still be there tomorrow when you wake. Sleep can realign your priorities and boost your spirit.

No matter how busy you get, take time to de-stress. Good ideas come when they are not beleaguered by your to-do list. Everyone's brain, including yours, deserves breaks and sometimes a mini vacation. Great leaders know how to Relax, Refuel, and Reload.

### #3: Keep your presence and heart in your home port.

If you've ever been on a cruise, you likely know that there are two types of ports. There's a home port and many call ports. A home port is where the boat starts and

> Great leaders know how to Relax, Refuel, and Reload.

ends. A call port is where passengers can get off to sight-see and then re-board to go to the next call port.

Many traveling leaders go through life experiencing mainly call ports and lose sight of their home port. I once sat listening to a very successful commercial pilot who was heading to divorce court for the third time. Tears rolled as he pleaded, "I've always excelled at my job, so why can't I keep a marriage together? I never want to go through this kind of pain again."

For every birth order, the very traits or abilities that enable you to succeed at work can exacerbate problems at home. That's why it's critical to not only know your strengths but how to use them in a way that builds up rather than tears down relationships.

## Thoughts of a Successful Leader

Change will not come if we wait for
some other person or some other time.
We are the ones we've been waiting for.
We are the change that we seek.

Barack Obama, 44th President of the United States

Consider Elena, the hard-working firstborn who just pushed through a huge project. Elated, she arrives home to a surprise party her young children have worked hard to put together for her. She scans the table, decked out in its created-by-kid finery. The attention-to-detail traits that helped her nail that award-winning project are still in high gear.

What's the first thing Elena says to her smiling 10-year-old firstborn daughter? "Oh, you forgot the napkins."

Think for a minute. Is it a mortal sin to not have napkins at a table? Isn't the joy on those kids' faces worth potentially having to use the edge of the tablecloth for a napkin and throwing that tablecloth in the wash? Or even throwing caution to the wind and having greasy or sticky fingers during that party?

What could Elena have said to use her detail-oriented nature to grow her relationships? "Oh, look at those beautiful cupcakes with the handmade stars on toothpicks. How did you guys figure out how to make frosting? And wow, the glitter on the tablecloth! So pretty. I see you also found the plastic mugs and plates we use when we go camping and make all those fun memories. What a surprise! You worked so hard to put this together. How creative and wonderful. This means so much to me. I can't wait to enjoy it together. Is it okay if I sit down and dive in? It looks so good!"

Or what about Jerrold, a lastborn who loves to throw impromptu get-togethers but forgets to tell his more reclusive middleborn housemate? That partner is enjoying homemade chicken cacciatore that's taken hours to make when those par-tygoers show up on the doorstep…before Jerrold arrives home.

But what if Jerrold had looped that housemate in a week earlier about wanting to have friends over? They could have planned it for an evening that worked for both of them. At the very least, Jerrold should have texted a heads-up and an apology when he remembered on his way home that he'd invited people over without asking the one most impacted by the event.

Or what about Elias, an only child who worked his way up the ladder into a substantial paycheck because of his detailed research ability? At work, he's respected for accumulating facts and drilling through them to find the best approach to a prob-lem. He arrives home to find an updated living room couch and a middleborn spouse who isn't typically a spender brimming with excitement.

"Doesn't it look nice?" she says. "It was right in our price range, and in a color I knew you'd like."

"Where did you get it?" he replies, still trying to get his head around the fact that there's a new piece of furniture sud-denly in the house. For the next five minutes, he grills her on the details including its place of manufacture, the research she did on fabrics and price points, etc. Her smile dims. The relational temperature that night resembles that of the Arctic.

What should Elias have done? He should have focused on what was important to that middleborn. Clearly she worked hard to find the best couch she could at a price range and color she knew he'd be comfortable with. He might want to try smiling and forming the words, "Wow, you're right. It does look nice. I loved that old couch, but this one makes the whole room look new. And the color is great. Thanks, honey, for making it happen."

The best advice I can give firstborns and onlies who are going home to someone is, "If you can't say something nice, don't say anything at all." A critical eye won't win friends or the cooperation of family members. Comments like "And the point of this story is…?" or "Could you get to the highlights?" won't either. Sometimes there's no end goal or point to a story. You merely need to sit back and enjoy the perspective you're gaining.

The best advice I can give to middleborns is, "What you think and feel matters." Yes, you are a peacemaker and negotiator at heart. You don't share easily because you don't want to ruffle anyone's feathers. But not sharing what is important to you will cause heartburn and heartache. You need to know that it's not only okay but very important for you to speak up and nicely set some parameters so others don't walk all over you.

The best advice I can give to lastborns is, "Not everyone wants a party 24/7." Even though you're not a big planner, those at home deserve respect and an extension of common courtesy. Let them know what's going on in your head and get their feedback before you act.

All birth orders need to practice the routine of turning off the distractions of work and turning on thoughts of home and family at the end of their workday. Use your drive home to transition from work thoughts to home thoughts. If you work from

> Best advice to firstborns and onlies:
> "If you can't say something nice, don't say anything at all."
>
> Best advice to middleborns:
> "What you think and feel matters."
>
> Best advice to lastborns:
> "Not everyone wants a party 24/7."

home, take a brisk walk around the block and clear your head before you engage with those you serve at home.

Your partner deserves your time and your full engagement. Your kids need to not only know you care but to also see and feel your affection in the form of time, attention, and priorities. When you blow it, those who matter most need to hear those magic words I talked about earlier: "I'm sorry. I was wrong. Please forgive me." Contrary to popular opinion, those words won't kill you. In fact, they can have a tremendous healing effect as long as you follow them up with altering the way you approach such a situation in the future.

If you can't admit your mistakes at home, how can you do it successfully anywhere else? Why not practice such skills with the people who matter most?

### #4: Choose a long-range perspective on failure and success.

A basketball coach nicknamed "The Wizard of Westwood" once lifted the UCLA Bruins from a struggling program to 10 championships in 12 years including seven in a row. That revered coach, John Wooden, would also lead the Bruins to an 88-game winning streak. But you know something? Over the 27 seasons

> "I'm sorry. I was wrong. Please forgive me." Contrary to popular opinion, those words won't kill you.

that Wooden coached that team, he never once told his team to go out and win. He told them to play the game of basketball the way it should be played.

When his teams went into big games, he didn't give motivational speeches. He would simply tell them, "I prepared you during the week. Now, do your job." He concentrated on developing his players to the best of their ability. "Don't try to be somebody else," he'd tell them. "You have to be yourself at all times."[30]

### Thoughts of a Successful Leader

Be more concerned with your character
than your reputation, because your character
is what you really are, while your reputation
is merely what others think you are.

JOHN WOODEN, AMERICAN BASKETBALL COACH

Life is full of events you can't control. But in every situation, there are things you *can* control. You can do your work to the best of your ability. You can live by your core values. You can choose to view failure and success with a long-range perspective.

When difficult events happen, leaders typically choose one of two paths. The first heads downward to a pity party *par excellence*. It's a steep trail complete with roots, rocks, and vines that trip you up. It focuses on what went wrong until you tumble into a muddy pit. "Why me?" you say, looking up at the darkening sky. "What did I ever do to deserve this?"

As you sit there, you beat yourself up. *There must have been something I did wrong, or this wouldn't have happened.* When you've expended that energy, you pass the blame onto others. *If only she wouldn't have…* or *I told him not to….* Neither attempt gets you out of that mud bath and back into civilization.

The second path starts with a reality check. *Wow, I certainly didn't expect this to happen. This is really rough.* Instead of allowing negative thinking to kick in, you evaluate the situation.

*We've had times like this before, and we've been able to come back strong. I have a great team. We have a hard work ethic and have each others' backs. We know what it's like to work 60-hour weeks when we have to.*

You get up and brush yourself off. *This derailment is major. It might take a couple 80-hour weeks to turn things around. But I know we can do it. No one's ever accused this team of being slackers.* You chuckle as you step back onto the path.

### Thoughts of a Successful Leader

I can't change the direction of the wind,
but I can adjust my sails to always reach my destination.

JIMMY DEAN, AMERICAN BUSINESSMAN, TV HOST, COUNTRY SINGER

Next steps crowd your thoughts now. *We'll need some help since I can't juggle overseeing all the extra work myself. Who would be best to lead a portion of this project, so we can tag-team? Might someone already on my team be eager to learn more about management? Or should we network with a trusted freelancer?*

Before you know it, the mental fog of impending doom and failure has cleared. You power back toward work because now you've got a plan. You're ready to rally the team that you know you can count on. Even if it takes those longer work weeks for a while, you're confident your team can get the project back on track.

You see, great leaders never give up. When one way doesn't work, they find another way. Failure doesn't mean an end or a lack of success. It means a redirection.

## Work It Out

Look at your definition for success from page 80. How might you change it now? What elements would you add? How about the ability to:

1. grow personal confidence along with your skills;

2. improve areas that aren't your strong suit;

3. choose your priorities wisely and stick to them;

4. provide value and benefit to others you serve and who serve with you;

5. see, find, and encourage the best in others;

6. learn from even the worst mistakes;

7. become a team player instead of a solo artist;

8. become emotionally resilient during difficult times; and

9. (add your own)?

Why not turn these into your very own "Success Checklist" to post where you'll see it often?

One of the simplest, most meaningful definitions of *success* I've ever heard came from a feisty 94-year-old great-grandma. She had lived through two world wars, a host of unusual work and pro-bono experiences, and more than her share of personal drama and trauma. "At the end of the day, can you look at yourself in the mirror and say, 'It's been a good day, hasn't it?' If you've remained true to all you hold dear, it *is* a good day."

Kudos to you, Great-grandma. We'd all do well to live up to that definition of *success,* wouldn't we?

### #5: Remember, leadership is personal.

I've highlighted this theme all throughout the book, but I'll say it again here. Leadership is personal. It's personal to you. It's personal to those you serve and who serve with you. It develops from the relationships you build at work, in your community, and at home. In an "it's all about me" culture, those who look for opportunities to encourage others, walk alongside them in mentoring, and invest in their lives will stand out greatly from the pack.

| Thoughts of a Successful Leader |
| --- |

Spoiler Alert: There are no relationships, careers,
or houses that can fill the hole.
There is nothing you can receive from the material
world that will create inner peace or fulfillment.
The truth is, "the Smile" is generated throughout output.
It is not something you get;
it's something you cultivate through giving.
In the end, it won't matter one single bit
how well [people] loved you.
You will only gain "the Smile"
based on how well you loved them.

Will Smith, American Actor, Film Producer

Over the last five days, this book has taken you on a journey. It started on Monday, with learning about birth order and how to maximize your strengths and shore up your weaknesses. On Tuesday, you looked at leadership traits and why balancing healthy authority and support with high expectations is so critical. On Wednesday, you discovered ways to motivate, problem-solve, and build beneficial relationships with those you serve. On Thursday, you examined the 5 P strategies that will help win cooperation. And on Friday, you learned how to communicate your purpose and intentionally craft your own unique culture.

Just look at what you've accomplished! That must feel really good. Combine those five winning plays and a growth mindset of lifelong learning—strengthened by aligned priorities, a healthy life balance, a heart and presence in your home port, and a long-range perspective on success—and your ability to change the world will be astounding.

Fast forward 10-20 years. You know who people will be talking about as the change-maker in their lives? The leader who believed in them, motivated them, and sparked their potential?

You.

# Top 15 Leader Countdown

15. Role-model hard work, respect, and the authoritative style.

14. Pursue excellence but never self-defeating perfection.

13. Maximize your strengths and shore up your weaknesses.

12. Refine your leadership traits with lifelong learning.

11. Remember the ABCs (Acceptance, Belonging, Competence).

10. Use the power of positive expectations and slather on the vitamins and virtues.

9. Observe and understand colleagues to ensure they're in the right seat on your bus.

8. Know those you serve and serve those you know.

7. Fine-tune strategies to win cooperation.

6. Intentionally craft your own unique culture.

5. Establish your core priorities and the rest will fall into place more easily.

4. Stay the course until the goal is accomplished.

3. Step back and de-stress when needed to get a fresh perspective.

2. Be grateful for every day and every new opportunity.

1. Remember: it's all about relationships.

# Notes

1    Alfred Adler, in P. Mairet, ed., *Problems of Neurosis* (New York, NY: Harper & Row Publishers, Inc., 1964).

2    Ibid.

3    Corinna Hartmann and Sara Goudarzi, "Does Birth Order Affect Personality?" *Scientific American,* Aug. 8, 2019, https://www.scientificamerican.com/article/does-birth-order-affect-personality/.

4    See Alfred Adler in P. Mairet, ed., op. cit., and Alfred Adler, *Understanding Human Nature* (New York: Fawcett World Library, 1927), 127.

5    Henry T. Stein, "Adlerian Overview of Birth Order Characteristics," *Classic Adlerian Depth Psychotherapy Institute,* http://www.adlerian.us/birthord.htm.

6    For more on birth order, see Dr. Kevin Leman, *The Birth Order Book: Why You Are the Way You Are* (Grand Rapids, MI: Revell, 1985, 1998, 2009).

7    Ibid.

8    "Leadership," *Merriam-Webster Dictionary,* https://www.merriam-webster.com/dictionary/leadership.

9    "Perfection," *Merriam-Webster Dictionary,* https://www.merriam-webster.com/dictionary/perfection.

10   Kenneth Labich, "Is Herb Kelleher America's Best CEO? Behind his clowning is a people-wise manager who wins where others can't," *CNN Business,* May 2, 1994, https://money.cnn.com/magazines/fortune/fortune_archive/1994/05/02/79246/index.htm.

11   Jackie Wattles, "Herb Kelleher, Southwest Airlines founder, dies at 87," *CNN,* Jan. 3, 2019, https://www.cnn.com/2019/01/03/business/southwest-airlines-founder-herb-kelleher-obit/index.html.

12   Ibid.

13   Kevin and Jackie Freiberg, "20 Reasons Why Herb Kelleher Was One of the Most Beloved Leaders of Our Time," *Forbes,* Jan. 4, 2019, https://www.forbes.com/sites/kevinandjackiefreib erg/2019/01/04/20-reasons-why-herb-kelleher-was-one-of-the-most-beloved-leaders-of-our-time/.

14   Ibid.

15   Ibid.

16   Jennifer Reingold, "Southwest's Herb Kelleher: Still crazy after all these years," *Fortune,* Jan. 14, 2013, https://fortune.com/2013/01/14/ southwests-herb-kelleher-still-crazy-after-all-these-years/.

17   Ibid.

18   "Today Show," *NBC,* 8:07 a.m., April 17, 2024, 8:07 a.m.

19   Kevin and Jackie Freiberg, op. cit.

20   Kyle Benson, "The Magic Relationship Ratio, According to Science," https://www.gottman.com/blog/ the-magic-relationship-ratio-according-science/.

21   Ibid.

22   "Praise," *Merriam-Webster Dictionary,* https://www.merriam-webster.com/dictionary/praise.

23   "Encouragement," *Oxford Languages,* https:///www.google.com/ search?q=encouragement+definition.

24   "Encourage," *Merriam-Webster Dictionary,* https://www.merriam-webster.com/dictionary/encourage.

25   Alfred Adler pioneered the idea of individual psychology in the 1920s. Later, American psychiatrist and educator Rudolf Dreikurs would develop that idea into a method for "understanding the purposes of misbehavior in children and stimulating cooperative behavior…..He described four 'mistaken goals' that…children would resort to and outlined the most effective ways that teachers

and parents could respond." See *New World Encyclopedia*, *Wikimedia* contributors, and Diana Lang, "1960s: Dreikurs," Iowa State University Digital Press, https://iastate.pressbooks.pub/parentingfamilydiversity/chapter/dreikurs/.

26  For more about the goals and stages of misbehavior, see Dr. Kevin Leman, *Parenting the Powerful Child* (Grand Rapids, MI: Revell, 2014).

27  "World War II Major Events Timeline," *PBS*, https://www.pbs.org/wgbh/masterpiece/specialfeatures/world-war-ii-major-events-timeline/#.

28  Winston Churchill, "Never Give In, Never, Never, Never, 1941," *America's National Churchill Museum*, https://www.nationalchurchillmuseum.org/never-give-in-never-never-never.html.

29  Caitlin Dempsey, "The Largest Cactus in the United States," *Geographyrealm*, https://www.geographyrealm.com/the-largest-cactus-in-the-united-states/#.

30  "John Wooden On College Basketball's Lost Beauty," Mar. 30, 2007, "Morning Edition," *NPR*, https://www.npr.org/2007/03/30/9215993/john-wooden-on-college-basketballs-lost-beauty.

## About Dr. Kevin Leman

An internationally known psychologist, radio and television personality, educator, speaker, and humorist, Dr. Kevin Leman has taught and entertained audiences worldwide with his wit and commonsense psychology.

The *New York Times* bestselling and award-winning author of over 70 titles on parenting, marriage, family, and education, including *The Birth Order Book, Have a New Kid by Friday, Sheet Music, Making Children Mind without Losing Yours, Parenting the Powerful Child, Be the Dad She Needs You to Be, The Way of the Shepherd, 8 Secrets to Raising Successful Kids, 7 Things He'll Never Tell You but You Need to Know, Why Kids Misbehave,* and *Planet Middle School,* Dr. Leman has made thousands of house calls through radio and television programs, including *FOX & Friends,* Hallmark Channel's *Home & Family, The View,* FOX's *The Morning Show, Today,* Dr. Bill Bennett's *Morning in America, The List, Today, Oprah, The 700 Club,* CBS's *The Early Show,* CNN, and *Focus on the Family.*

Dr. Leman has served as a contributing family psychologist to *Good Morning America.* He frequently speaks to schools, CEO groups, businesses—including Fortune 500 companies and others such as YPO, Million Dollar Round Table, and Top of the Table—and civic and church organizations. A practicing psychologist for over 40 years, Dr. Kevin Leman has helped millions of adults understand the dynamics of healthy relationships.

His professional affiliations include the American Psychological Association and the North American Society of Adlerian Psychology. He received the Distinguished Alumnus Award (1993) and an honorary Doctor of Humane Letters degree (2010) from North Park University, and a bachelor's degree in psychology, and later his master's and doctorate degrees, as well as the Alumni Achievement Award (2003)—the highest award they can give one of their own—from the University of Arizona. Dr. Leman is the founder and chairman of the governing board of Leman Academy of Excellence (www.lemanacademy.com).

Originally from Williamsville, New York, Dr. Leman and his wife, Sande, live in Tucson, Arizona, and have five children and four grandchildren.

If you're looking for an entertaining speaker for your event or fund-raiser, or for information regarding business consultations, webinars, or the annual "Wit and Wisdom" cruise, please contact:

Dr. Kevin Leman
PO Box 35370
Tucson, Arizona 85740
Phone: (520) 797-3830
www.birthorderguy.com

Follow Dr. Kevin Leman on Facebook (facebook.com/DrKevinLeman) and on X (@DrKevinLeman). Check out the free podcasts at birthorderguy.com/podcast.

For "Dr. Kevin Leman" resources on marriage, parenting, family, and many other topics: go to amazon.com.

For more about Leman Academy of Excellence visit lemanacademy.com.